AF481129

ETERNAL LOVING

Inspiring Conscious Relationship as a Path for Masculine/Feminine Embodiment and Spiritual Awakening

JOHNNY BLACKBURN

Eternal Loving

Editor: Melanie Buntin

Front cover image source: Shutterstock

Back cover author's photo: Josh McMurtrie

This addition is printed on acid-free paper that meets the American National Standards Institute Standard.

Printed and Bound in the United States of America

Presence Academy, Inc.
San Diego, California

First Printing, 2024

DEDICATION

To all us humans
learning to give and receive love,
while opening as
Awake Love.

Table of Contents

The Lovers

The Relating

GRATITUDE & ACKNOWLEGEMENT

ABOUT THE AUTHOR

Introduction

Relationship as a Spiritual Practice

In centuries past, romantic relationships were commonly viewed as an alternative to a spiritual life. There are a variety of reasons that a life of spiritual depth in past eras involved a retreat from the world. Perhaps much of what was cultivated by these ancient mystics, the giants on whose shoulders we stand, was actually in preparation for a time in the future—a time like now. We find ourselves alive in a time when the conscious development of humanity has 1) reached a critical mass: 2) when spirituality can safely be practiced and expressed without persecution, and 3) when global communication channels allow its spread beyond local in-person teachings. As a result of the convergence of these factors, personal and spiritual development can now effectively be integrated into every aspect of our lives, at work and especially in relationships. In some ways, conscious romantic partnership may actually now be one of the most potent spiritual development containers of our times.

Too often we allow the new relationship emotions of the honeymoon phase to be the primary driver ushering us into relationships. However, without having some essential conscious relationship skills and a developmental orientation, many of us then plummet from those highs as soon as the committed relationship phase begins when unconscious patterns of behavior arise. Many of us shut down, pull away or justify behaviors when disconnection occurs, miscommunication happens or past patterns play out.

Without a growth-mindset and the context of partnership as a spiritual practice, many of us don't engage our romantic relationship as an invitation and opportunity to continue to heal, develop and Awaken spiritually. Romantic relationships can be so challenging and can be the source of so much pain. But they can also be the source of some of our most beautiful moments and an amplifying catalyst for so much growth: personally, relationally and spiritually.

As a spiritual practice, our partnership can be a profound teacher and reflective mirror, helping us become more self-aware and be more loving. This journey of conscious relationships may involve healing our past, developing ourselves personally, embodying virtues, learning to communicate, becoming more securely attached, learning emotional intelligence, strengthening trust, magnetizing attraction with polarity, becoming able to repair conflict and reconnect, cultivating presence and evolving our sexuality so that love making and our entire relationship becomes a spiritual practice.

Beyond the romance glorified in codependent love songs or the lack thereof in disconnected lifeless marriages, there exist some brave and bright souls who remember that Love is the essence of Life. They know, and, more importantly, feel the love when their hearts are open. These ambassadors of love also understand that their romantic partner is their chosen practice partner (and in reality, all their relationships), to walk through infinity together, for some amount of time. Both have, on some level of their beings, agreed to help remind each other to open and reopen their hearts again and again in the process of growing, loving and Awakening as Love Itself. As we deepen together, the more our partner can become our greatest source of support, our closest confidant, a polarity magnetizer and a consummate reminder to stay open, be loving and Awaken as Love.

Maybe, beyond just biological reproduction or social conventions, maybe, just maybe, we are here to grow, to deepen our capacity to love and to Spiritually Awaken. What if Ram Dass was right when he said: "We are all just walking each other home?" What if Love was the essence of Life and what if your, my and our human nervous systems were the instruments for the experience of learning to love and Being Love?

In the midst of it all, deep down, my love, this may be what we are doing here, together. And if so, we can co-create an ongoing romance, a long, slow, epic foreplay with presence and love in all the things, so that our relationship and entirety of our lives are a spiritual practice—knowing that our openness and the Love that loves through us is really an offering to You, Life

Readers' Note 1

56 Names of the Universe

What does it all mean? When you come across words that have the first letter capitalized, as in the case of the following terms, know that they are signifiers for the Universe.

Aliveness
All Things
Awake
Awake Love
Awake as All Things
Awakening
Awareness
Awareness Itself
Beauty Herself
Big Heart
Big Love
Big Mind
Creation
Divine
Divinity Herself
Empty Vastness
Essence
Eternal
Eternal Loving
Existence
Fabric of Reality
Grace
Great Chain of Being
Great Openness of Love
Great Mystery
Great She
I Am
Infinite

Life
Love
Love Being
Love Itself
Loving Awareness
Loving Awareness Itself
Non-Dual
Non-Duality
One
Oneness
Openness
Presence
Presence of Life
Radiance Herself
Reality
Source
Space
Spacious Awareness
The Field
The Moment
Transcendence
Totality of Now
True Freedom
True Essence
True Nature
Universe
You
Your Presence

READERS' NOTE 2

The Spectrum of Gender & Relationship Orientation

This book and its writings explore personal, relational and spiritual development through the container of romantic partnership. In some sections it speaks to masculine and feminine energies and qualities, offering perspectives on how they interact and influence relationships and life.

The terms "masculine" and "feminine" are used to describe archetypal qualities, also known as yang and yin, initiatory and receptive, etc. that can be embodied by anyone, regardless of gender identity or sexual orientation. These energies are part of a spectrum of polarity and are distinct from biology (male and female based on anatomy, genetics, and hormone levels) or identity (mental orientations based on beliefs, meaning-making and socially constructed concepts). While the primary emphasis in some sections may seem to be at times on masculine and feminine energies and associated qualities, this is not intended to exclude or diminish any gender orientations, identities, or fluid experiences.

Similarly, although most sections tend to relate to monogamous relationships, some of the dynamics can also apply or be modified for individuals in ethical non-monogynous, polyamorous or other creative relationship arrangements. We honor and respect all individuals, regardless of their gender identity or relationship orientation and we celebrate the diverse expressions of these energies.

The insights and discussions within these pages are offered as one perspective and are not meant to prescribe a singular way of being or relating. Understanding the spectrum of human relationships is essential to fostering inclusivity and mutual respect. Readers from all backgrounds and experiences are invited to reflect on these ideas and adapt them in ways that resonate with their own unique personal and relational journeys.

We hope this book offers valuable insights that positively contribute to your own embodiment of greater potential, more conscious relating and spiritual awakening, while appreciating the rich tapestry of human and spiritual experience.

Open To It

Love is an endless mystery, just like Life.
You don't have to fully understand to deeply experience it,
but you do have to open your heart.

PART 1

THE FEMININE

TENDERNESS

____

I had to pass through
the societal trappings
seeming to convince me
I am supposed to be tough
and not so "emotional".

In contorting and hardening
my natural essence
to fit the mold of belonging
I sacrificed my own acceptance:
disconnecting from myself
shutting down my feelings
hardening my face
building walls around my heart
and distancing it from you—
all to hide my tenderness.

All the times I've been
judged for vulnerability
dismissed in my feelings,
told to "stop crying" or
"fixed" to manage your discomfort,
have all contributed to me
not feeling fully safe
to be vulnerably open
revealing my tender underbelly
allowing the softest parts to be felt
and the most beautiful parts to be seen.

The scars from my past and
the walls I've built around my heart
conceal these parts of me
In some effort to keep me safe.
But they really just rob me
of the closeness and intimacy
I most deeply crave.

This is my heroine's journey
to reconnect to myself,
my innocent loving core,
to openly feel all the feels,
and let life touch me
through the tenderness
of my own beautiful heart.

Have you hardened yourself?
And if so, have you softened again
and refound your tender feminine core?

BEING SEEN

"If you really saw all of me",
she asked,
"would you still love me?"

She discovered
it was her own protectors
following the orders
they'd been given
to keep her safe
from hurt or judgment
overcast, a layer of subtle concealment
obscuring her deeper desire,
instead, guarding her from being seen.

"If you really saw all of me,"
she asked,
"would you still love me?"

Until that is,
the intensity of her Soul's yearning
and the beckoning warmth
from the light of the Source
became stronger
than her impulse to hide.

In a flash of evolutionary insight
she realized it was her own fear.
She was the one covering herself
the parts she tried to hide,
the things she felt ashamed of,
her fears and insecurities,
the parts she was still learning to accept.

And so...
she embraced her deepest desire
to be fully and deeply seen
allowing the beauty of

her unique Soul Essence and
the brightening rays of Grace
that animate through all things
to radiantly shine through her.
Just like the sun is still shining
even if there's some cloud cover
The Loving Acceptance that is
the very fabric of the Universe
never stopped embracing her.
She just had to let It in.

Is your desire to hide stronger than your desire to be seen?
What are some things you don't yet accept or don't want
others to see that may be inhibiting the natural urge of
your essence to be seen?

MESSINESS

I don't always have it all together.
And sometimes,
I don't feel beautiful.
And other times,
I feel like a mess.

I used to be afraid,
to let go of my composure.
I put this false pressure on myself,
because I didn't want to let you down.
And I felt like I couldn't let myself cry,
so I had to keep it all together.
What felt like a fear of judgment,
was really me judging myself,
and stifling the flow of Life,
through me.

But as wild and unbridled,
as emoting may seem to you,
I've learned to allow,
the flux and flow of moods,
a symphony of vulnerability,
tears cascading,
like a soft gentle rain,
or as a strong flood of feelings.

I realized what I thought,
was a break down,
was actually a crack open,
and how the light gets in.
Because sometimes
I just need to be held,
while weeping uncontrollably,
face smeared in snot and tears.

Far better
than a lifeless numbing,
or rigid buttoning-up,
I would never be as beautiful,
and emotionally open,
as I am,
if I didn't let the messiness
move through sometimes.

This messiness teaches me,
to embrace the chaos,
the courage to surrender,
the power in vulnerability,
the freedom in releasing,
and to truly accept,
all of me.

Allowing myself to feel
the full spectrum of emotions,
something more
opens within me,
something previously inaccessible,
the tender core of my heart,
where my true beauty shines,
and my loving essence lives.

BEAUTIFYING

What is the Source
of this beauty
that lives through you
and All Things?

Will you use it to capture attention
in striving to boost your own worth?
Or, fearing that the loss of beauty and youth
will somehow diminish your value,
allowing yourself to be lured and consumed
by the external efforts to enhance
while subconsciously striving to feel "enough",
overlooking the true Source of beauty within?

Or, will you continually soften open
allowing your essential desire
to beautify and adorn
yourself and others and let Life
shine freely through you
as you dress, do your makeup
decorate rooms and brighten spaces,
as you bless and better
all the things,
in beautifying
this amazing world?

*Do you make yourself up with the intention
of earning love, or do you beautify and adorn
yourself from a state of loving yourself?*

Soft to the Touch

As powerful and competent as I am,
I am also tender and loving inside.
I feel really deeply
and I am soft to the touch.

So if you want to experience
my caring and nurturing side,
don't dismiss my feelings or
talk to me like I'm one of the guys.

When I open my heart to you,
please treat me with the utmost respect.
Be loving and considerate of my heart.
And even if I am sometimes guarded
comin' in strong and sassy,
or I am being emotionally reactive,
underneath that tough exterior,
remember that I am
still soft to the touch.

Deep down,
I really just want to love
and be loved—
feeling emotionally safe,
so I can open with you
and have you accept me
in all my moments.

So, if you want to unlock
my deepest essence,
bring me your attuned presence
and please be patient with me,
because at the center of my heart,
I am soft to the touch.

DEVOTION

The heartbeat of perseverance:
devotion,
the silent force,
with a constancy of care,
helping her complete ordinary tasks
and tending to her deepest matters,
like an unwavering flame
lighting her way,
in faithful service,
dedicated
to living as love.

What do you care so much about
that you're willing to devote your life to?

CARING

You point us to what matters.
You inspire us to give attention.
You invite us to attune to what's needed.
You help us value and respect.
You animate us to nurture and protect.

You, guardian of well-being,
alchemizing tangible gestures
that heal, nourish and uplift.

You, accompaniment of loving,
who remind us we are not alone
on this journey of shared humanity.

What are some ways you take care of yourself?
What are some ways you could take better care of yourself?
What are some ways you can be more caring towards others?

NURTURING

You are like
a warm gentle rain
that washes away
the unneeded
and fills us up
with the essence of life.

Your affectionate care,
and attuned attention
behind your supportive acts
nourishes and enriches us–
loving us up
encouraging us to grow
and realize our potential.

Oh so beautiful,
the ways you
lovingly tend
and sustain
the miracle of life.

What are some ways you can be
more nurturing towards others?

WITH AND WITHOUT YOU

She does not need him,
but deep down,
she knows,
they amplify each other.

Yes, sometimes
her body craves
to melt into his strong arms;
at other times to flow on her own.

The more she feels him
in his presence, integrity and direction,
the more safety and trust gets created,
allowing her to soften open and glow.

The very qualities
the other naturally desires,
mutually inspires and
unlocks each others' best.
Sure she knows
she can take care of
and provide for herself
on her own.

And yet,
sometimes it feels really good,
to be able to allow someone else
she really deeply trusts
who also happens to be really sexy
to do certain things for her,
because he wants to
as a loving act of service.

And even if it feels easier
to soften more deeply open
with him in her life,
she also knows,

those same channels exist inside her,
which certain people
or situations can activate,
but that ultimately
exist within.
So, she continues
to focus on loving herself
and opening her pathways,
feeling and releasing all her emotions,
allowing pleasure to animate her body,
whether together or in solitude.

She realizes the more she is in flow,
the more her body relaxes open,
the more radiant she is,
the more Love Itself
can shine through,
regardless of her relationship status.
And so, she practices softening open,
whether she is with or without you.

Do you allow yourself to be open-hearted
and loving with those close to you?
Are you able to feel open-hearted love
when no one else is around?

Being Led

Is it possible that your desire
for his clear, trustable direction,
parallels your yearning for Life,
to gracefully guide you,
through synchronicity and flow,
amidst this Great Mystery.

So what if,
the leading and being led,
your learning to trust,
as he maintains trustworthiness:
strong, centered and open
so you can soften to him,
in the great human dance
was ultimately
a space to practice
surrendering to the Divine,
as a loving feminine being
and into your True Nature
Loving Awareness Itself.

How are you at trusting and
allowing your partner to lead you?
How are you at trusting and
allowing Life to guide you?

Hey Beautiful

Have I told you
how beautiful,
I find you, lately?
It doesn't
have anything to do
with your make-up,
your new clothes
or your weight.

Yes, I love when you
adorn yourself,
stylize your wardrobe
and take care of your health.
But these external things
just illuminate the inner.

And, conversely, small blemishes
are but tiny specks
on the surface of the Sun
whose radiant light
gives life to all living things
on this planet.

Deep down,
I know you know
the true Source of your beauty
meets at the intersection
of your human form,
Soul Essence
and Divinity Herself.

When you allow yourself
to be emotionally open
and to really be seen
in all your states of being,
from vulnerable messiness
to elegant excellence,

it is there that
Beauty Herself
shines through.
And from this space
your beauty and its adornments
are acts of loving offering
to yourself, to me and to Life.

HOW WOULD YOU BREATHE?

Read this and tell me:
how would you breathe,
if you were being made love to,
slowly and deeply,
right
this
very
moment?

How much deeper
would your breath be,
in the full openness
of your body's pleasure,
than how
it is
right
now?

What if the Presence of Life,
that always surrounds you,
was trying to
to make love to you;
not undressing you,
but opening you,
into the bliss,
of Existence Itself?

What if, rather than,
being habitually clenched closed,
numbing your emotions,
suppressing past trauma,
guarding your heart to avoid hurt,
or withholding love to punish him,
you embraced Life's natural invitations,
to open you,
to animate you
with Love?

Just know, you can.
Just know, you are free,
to open or close,
as desired.
Just know, the same Aliveness,
that lives in All Things,
that creates through you,
and grows life in you,
is also breathing you.

So, now, how would you breathe?

Pleasure Novas

So close and connected,
deeper and deeper,
more and more open,
building and building,
until a massive peak
with multiple waves of crescendos,
an explosion of climactic pleasure,
like ecstatic supernovas of bliss,
radiating outward
from the center of your cervix,
as the middle of The Moment,
from your Soul Essence,
as an offering to Existence.
May the pleasure and love
that move through you,
over-flowingly brighten,
and beautify All Things.

CERVICALS

So, let's talk about the cervix.
Now, I am not referring to
laying on some cold metal table,
in some sterile office
while someone,
definitely not your lover
cranks you open
to take a look.

We've all heard of
and, hopefully you've enjoyed,
the peak pleasure
of the clitoral and g-spot climaxes,
but have you ever experienced
a cervical orgasm?

I mean have you ever
felt so emotionally safe,
so connected,
so surrendered open,
your body as relaxed as it has ever been,
so filled with energy and aliveness
that the immensity of pleasure,
many magnitudes greater
than your average blissful climax,
exploded like a supernova star of ecstasy,
rippling goodness outward,
from the center of your being
radiating to all of Creation.

*Could this sacred experience from the
center of your being be many magnitudes
greater than a quick surface release?*

At the Core of Your Yearning

What do you yearn for
at the center of your being?

What do you feel inside
if you get still, quiet and listen?

I imagine the surface of the longing
can be really painful,
so it's sometimes easier to distract,
rather than feel into the center of it.

But if you really feel it,
in the center of your heart,
as long as it needs to be felt,
without avoiding, unfiltered
by mental interpretation,
simply present with the pure sensations
it will reveal itself.
Then, you might discover
it has been a feeling
you have been avoiding,
or unwilling to meet
inhibiting you this whole time.

Maybe part of you doubts
if you really deserve to
receive your desire,
or you falsely fear
that if you feel it,
it'd be too intense or never end.

Or are you not allowing
yourself really want it,
to prevent a possible disappointment
if by chance you don't get it?
For it is by this very act
of meeting, feeling and appreciating

these feelings and protectors,
that you help them relax and release.
And if you truly allow yourself
to feel it all the way to the center,
the transmission of the ache
becomes the reciprocal homing signal
beckoning and magnetizing
what you desire to you
and leading you into
the depths of your Being.

So those deeply, devoted beings
who courageously feel
all the way through to the center
find a secret treasure.
Amidst the powerful vulnerability
there lies their tender humanness
and Love Itself at the core.

RADIANCE

She yearns to soften open,
while she learns to allow
the aliveness of Life
to gracefully move through her
as she feels and releases
all her emotions,
now free,
and flowing with devotion
so the radiant beauty of Existence
can shine through her essence
animated by Love Itself.

Uncontained

Are you having difficulty
fitting me in a box?
Very well then,
I Am Infinite,
the boundless and uncontainable,
that animates all things.

"Do I contradict myself?
Very well then I contradict myself,
I am vast, I contain multitudes."

—— Walt Whitman ——
Leaves of Grass

PART 2

THE MASCULINE

PURPOSE

Why are you here?

What's yours to contribute?

Who are you here to be
and what do you need to do
to become that?

What matters to you so much
that you are willing
to dedicate your life to
or give your life for?

Do you have the courage
to ask yourself these deeper questions?
Not just to mentally understand the concepts,
but to venture into the uncertain depths
of this great mystery
to discover the deeper wisdom
and develop yourself
until you and your life
have become the living answer.

Are you willing to accept
your own hero's quest?

Why are you here?

What is your purpose?
If you don't know, what are
you doing to discover it?

Contribution

What are your unique strengths and talents?

What limits, stifles or holds you back?

What weaknesses and blindspots get in your way?

What skills have you been developing?

What are your superpowers to unleash?

What is yours to do while here?

How do you feel inspired to contribute
to the evolution of our world
making it even more
knowledgeable,
functional,
sustainable,
beautiful,
truthful,
ethical,
loving
&
Awake?

What is yours to contribute
to make the world better,
brighter and more beautiful?

GRIT

Not all smooth and shiny.

An inner strength
seasoned with character.
Persevering in the face
of adversity and obstacles.

When the going gets tough,
grit fuels you to keep going
when you get knocked down,
grit gets you back up again.

It is a tenacious determination
plus a growth mindset.
Courageous resilience
with a thirst for betterment.

A measure of how you
deal with failure,
learn from your mistakes
and use them to keep improving.

Raw talent is good to start with,
but by itself doesn't mean much.
Talent plus practice builds skill,
and skill plus grit leads to mastery.

DEDICATION

Where weakness collapses,
and flakiness falters,
there is a strength
and steadiness
in true dedication.

Not burdensome duty,
or mundanely ticking off another task,
but aligned with higher principles
and guided by deeper motivation.

Not quitting when challenged,
nor floundering in excuses,
the loyalty to your commitments
animates the drive
and fuels the perseverance
to work months, even years
to achieve your goals
never losing sight
of the deeper purpose
and the objects of
your dedication.

Making sure it's handled,
day in and day out,
whatever is needed,
with unwavering resolve,
it will be protected,
provided,
and with dedication
it will get done.

*What matters so much to
you that you'd dedicate your
life to or give you life for?*

Consistency

Do you show up for your people?

And do you show up for your commitments?

It starts the first hour of every day
how you activate each morning,
by doing your practices
getting centered,
and powering up
so you can show up
resourced and resourceful,
strong and steady.

Consistency
is the self-discipline
to take consistent action
step by step,
task by task,
getting things done
at work and at home,
to complete projects
to handle things
and reach your goals.

It continues,
with how on point you live,
how you stay accountable,
ways you eat, train, sleep,
mastering your habits
and using your arsenal
to manage yourself,
your stress,
responsibilities
and your life.

And if we asked her
whether you were consistent,

what would she say?
Are you present with her, with your life?
Are you emotionally available
and open so she can connect with you?
Are you able to self-regulate
and stay centered so she can share her feelings?
Are you steady so she can depend on you;
there for her when she needs you?

Not bored by routine,
but fueled by dedication,
clear on your priorities,
moving towards targets
completing tasks and projects
showing up to your commitments,
regardless of circumstance.
It's not about some idealized perfection,
rigid, controlled predictability,
or some kind of static balance.

Life is dynamic,
and evolving.
Be like Bruce Lee and the water,
composed under pressure,
staying centered in upheaval,
resilient amidst challenge,
still getting it done,
day in and day out.

If you fall off
trust yourself to
get back up,
get back to it,
get back on point,
and pick up where you left off,
in steadfast pursuit,
you continue your consistency.

It's not from burden or fearing mistakes;
but for the love of the game,

making the masterpiece of your life
even more badass.
Own your life,
aim high,
strive for betterment,
learn consistency,
cultivate virtues
and thrive
all throughout your life.

CHALLENGE

In the face of challenge,
you become better and stronger.
In the heat of its fire,
your character is forged.

Part of you feels
most alive and fulfilled
when facing competition
discovering what you are capable of
and overcoming obstacles
toward the realization
of your goals
and the actualization
of your potential.

Along the way,
you may get injured or sick
but you can recover.
It might get messy,
but you can clean it up.
Life might knock you down,
but you can get back up.

Your lover
is probably going to test you,
but it is her process of trusting
and surrendering open to you.

If you open your heart to love,
it might get hurt,
but you can heal it, reopen
and love even more.

Your ego
might get bruised,
but it is helping you to be humble
and bow down to Life.

Things might not always be smooth
and may not go your way,
but you can persevere
and cultivate composure.

Life may take away
people and things
you really care about,
but it's teaching you
to love while fully engaged,
amidst impermanence.

There will be
a whole range of things
beautiful and tragic,
all of which are empowering you
to be strong and stay upright
in the face of adversity.
Ultimately, Life challenges you
to embody presence and freedom
in the engagement
all throughout your life.

Your loved ones and Life
beckon you forward
into the fray
challenging you to live
at the edge of your growth
as the evolutionary urge
of Life Itself
evolves through you.

*Do you tend to collapse under challenge
or do you use it to strengthen and grow?*

ENGAGEMENT

"Engage Maverick, engage!"

You can watch from your couch,
and pretend on your VR headset.
You can zone out, numb out
or escape into the fantasies
to distract from the pain
of a disengaged life.

Or you can get up,
roll up your sleeves
and get in the game, man.
Do you have the courage
to be engaged in real life,
to show up for yourself
and your future?

Are you willing to grow,
and face challenges,
get knocked down
and get back up,
fail and triumph
while living fully
along the way.

Have you heard the whispers
that have been calling you,
inviting you into
your own hero's quest?

Our world needs
the best version of you
and your positive contribution.
Quit fucking around,
engage
and do
what you
came here
to do.

Integrity

There is deep honor
in living a life with integrity.

It is not a fixed thing
that once demonstrated,
is done and can be forgotten about.
It is not automatically granted,
nor something you can buy.

Integrity is a virtue,
to be cultivated and maintained,
that builds confidence and trust
within oneself and from others.
It requires and emanates
strength of character.

It is an inner compass
for living in alignment with
values, words and actions
and a soul's true north,
guiding our way to
the ultimate alignment
with something greater.

Integrity is something earned,
it can be cleaned up and rebuilt,
or it can also be easily lost
when we are out of alignment,
unskillful or unconscious.
So it makes it that much more
special and worthy of respect
when you meet someone
who embodies integrity.

May he strive to align
his words, actions, values and choices.

May he honor his word.

May he speak to others
as he wants to be spoken to.

May he treat others
as he wants to be treated.

May he do what he says he will do
and follow through on commitments
or request an amendment.

May he take accountability
for the impact of his actions
on self, others and world.

May he take ownership
and responsibility for his life.

May he continue to strive to live
with ever more integrity.

*What's the area of your life in which you
are out of integrity and what's one
thing you can do to restore it?*

Integrity Inspirer

When you follow through
on something you said you'd do
whether a seemingly small thing
like taking out the trash
or something significant in your life,
your integrity is a big deal
for your romantic partner.

All those moments are either
building or damaging your integrity.
Most men don't understand
how this indirectly impacts
how much she trusts you,
allows herself to be led
and surrender open to you.

But since she likely wants you
to grow and approach
the best version of yourself
her desire for your integrity,
which just happens to be
intertwined with her trust in you,
is not just nagging or complaint,
but is actually encouraging your betterment.

It may initially start as
an external motivation,
until you take ownership of your life
strive to live with integrity yourself
and want to develop it as a virtue,
even when nobody is looking.

So, it might help you to remember
that the beautiful, and at times challenging,
integrity inspirer that is your partner,
is actually an emissary of the Divine,

a messenger of Life Itself in human form,
inviting you to live in alignment, virtue
and to move towards the best version of you.

RELIABILITY

I highly value your trust
and ability to depend on me.
I understand that
how I show up for you
is ever contributing to
or weakening your
ability to rely on me.

When I am more centered,
the more I can be relied on.
I've learned to self-regulate,
healthfully manage stress
and be consistent in my
daily morning practices
to stay centered,
aligned, grounded,
composed and expansive.

When I am living in integrity
the more I can be relied on.
I strive to live aligned with my
values, words and actions.
And I work to restore or repair
when there is incoherence.

When I am willing to grow,
the more I can be relied on.
I may not be perfect,
but I'm willing to be humble,
honestly acknowledge
where I have room to grow
and take actions accordingly
to continue to do so.
When I undefendedly receive feedback
on a request you make
and actually implement it
as well as improve over time,
it only enhances my reliability.

When I am emotionally mature
the more I can be relied on.
When my emotional intelligence
allows me to stay present, open
and composed so you can co-regulate,
when I listen without trying to fix,
when I acknowledge my impact,
when I sincerely apologize
and make amends when off,
I imagine you can rely on me more.

When I am available to connect
the more I can be relied on.
I have consciously chosen you,
I am here and not going anywhere.
I can sense when something feels off
and communicate until it's repaired.
I positively respond when you reach for connection,
so you feel safer and relax more deeply
into your feminine essence
and so I can create security overall
in our romantic relationship.

So because of all those impacts,
but even more so for myself,
for the cultivation of virtue
and pursuit of my greater potential.
I strive to be a solid, steady,
grounded pillar of reliability
in all areas of my life while
keeping the joy, aliveness and playfulness.

FREEDOM

———————

There is this strong drive deep inside
to seek and find freedom,
If you really pause to sense it,
you notice it has been here all along.

He has been testing limits since he was two.
And when he was more implosive
he thought freedom was being able
to do what he wanted, when he wanted.
Part of him wanted to be free of rules,
free of outside limits and restraints.
He feared commitment; it might tie him down.
So he devised all kinds of subtle ways to escape.

As he got a little older, he thought maybe
it was financial freedom he sought
so, he took a job he didn't really like
and started working long hours.
If he made lots of money and
retired early then maybe
he'd finally feel free, he hoped.

He worked more hours, managed more people,
plus marriage, house, kids and all the things,
but nothing gave fulfillment and he still wasn't free.
Only now he'd lost the joy—
filled with stress and burden.
drinking too much hoping to feel better,
but really just numbing out.

Where was this elusive freedom he had been ever seeking?

Until one day a friend suggested he try meditation.
At first, he scoffed at the idea and was resistant,
but eventually he acknowledged that
what he was doing wasn't working.
So, he was willing to give something new a try.

Initially, he found it difficult trying to sit still.
His mind was busy and his body uncomfortable.
He kept at it though and started to improve.
All of a sudden one morning on the cushion,
the thoughts fell away and his mind went very quiet.
He kept practicing focusing his attention
and learned how to free it from thought.

Then he started working with a somatic therapist
and learned to open his heart,
so he was once again free to feel joy.
This guide also introduced him to partswork,
helping him be more integrated and
free to authentically express himself.
When he used to use alcohol,
to knock out his inhibiting protectors,
he now learned to relax with awareness.
And then he learned how to relax all the parts,
the very sense of self, revealing the True Freedom
now open as Awareness Itself.

When he was young, he used to
seek freedom from externals.
Now he realizes freedom is an inside job—
moment to moment.
It is the True Freedom that's been
beckoning this whole time.
Stabilizing free in the midst
of human life. This is his practice.

"Emancipate yourself from mental slavery"

—— Bob Marley ——
Redemption Song

Learn to meditate to free your mind.

Upright & Uncollapsing

Of course she doesn't like getting angry.
She'd much rather be laughing or loving,
but if she is mad at least she is alive.

And even if she won't admit it,
there may have been a time or two,
when she sparked a conflict just so
she can feel you emotionally open.

Other times, the nature of the feminine
can be overtaken by a storm
as she unleashes her fire upon you
a subconscious test just to see
if you'll collapse or lose your composure.

Or can you remain
unwavering in presence
looking her in the eyes,
calling her by name
and letting her know
it's okay she's mad
before inviting her back into love.

She melts in your arms as she weeps
in the indirect realization
of how much more deeply
she can trust him.

Nature is very powerful,
in case you haven't noticed
and so is your Presence
if you have the courage
to discover and develop it.

He's Got Her

It is said to be a deep feminine pleasure
to be picked up and carried into the bedroom
before making passionate love.
Some women may also like it
when in the midst of conversation,
he smoothly, yet suddenly
pins her against the wall,
pausing for a moment,
pervading her with presence,
then slowly kissing her,
before stepping back and
returning to the conversation
as if nothing happened–
without wanting anything more.

And while these smooth and sexy
masculine demonstrations of
physical strength, sexiness and presence
can be fun, passionate and romantic,
there is a lot more depth to it.
Ask your feminine partner
if it is true for her,
that deep down, at her core
she wants to feel through and through
that "you've got her"
in several important ways.

For her to soften
and deeply open
through her body
as her radiant loving essence
she first needs to feel
physically safe with you.
This involves your physical strength,
embodied physicality and competence.
This allows you to physically protect her
from the outside world, if ever needed,

while also maintaining safety within
by never physically harming her.
Now of course,
she can take care of herself,
so she might not 'need' you,
but she might feel even more safe
knowing she can fully relax into
your all-encompassing protection.

This gets to the very essence
of how you inhabit your physicality,
move through the world
defend yourself and her,
and confidently handle a situation.
It also shows up in how you
grab and hold her hand,
walk with her on the street,
and ensure she is safe at night.

Now in terms of the protection
in being a provider,
in the old times,
providing for your partner and family
was about being a good hunter,
which was a matter of survival.
And while much of humanity
is still in survival mode,
or subsistence farming,
for some living in modern economies
providing a quality standard of living
is a form of masculine love.
More than just picking up the tab
or paying the electric bills,
it's a way of taking care of her
and demonstrating you've got her,
that she can trust your stewardship
as well as the security of the life
you are leading her into.

And lastly there's the safety
in your emotional presence.

She will want to feel
and have you prove,
sometimes through testing,
that you can stay present
in the face of her emotions.
This means that you won't
easily collapse as she emotes,
gaslight or dismiss her feelings,
or get stuck up in your mind
overusing logic or hyper-rationality
to avoid your own feelings.
It means you won't get uncomfortable,
and try to fix or cheer her up,
shut down, numb, guard your heart or
have low emotional intelligence,
only able to express anger and frustration.
it means you can read and stay present with,
name, feel and release,
the whole range within her and you.
She wants to feel you, man,
through the openness of your heart,
to the depths, in each moment.
Of course, don't be a stoic robot.
If something gets triggered in you,
rather than collapsing, reacting,
or getting aggressive,
can you stay open and vulnerable,
centered and empowered,
while working to release it,
and restore mutual connection?
Your task to master is
to stay relaxed, grounded, open and present
in the face of whatever she is expressing,
but not beyond the point of
enabling her to be verbally violent.
If she starts getting overly aggressive,
critical, and emasculating,
can you respect yourself
and stay empowered enough
to redirect her misguided attempts
back to presence and love?

She may be unconsciously acting out
her past pain and unresolved trauma,
frustrated that you are not
more open to connection
or subconsciously testing you
to see if are you strong enough to
stay centered without collapsing,
so she can surrender open to you.
For her to really trust you deeply,
you must demonstrate
through your emotional presence
that you've really got her.

"I've got you" is now often overused.
It doesn't just mean
you'll pay the dinner bill
or you can pick her up
and carry her to bed.
Deep down she likely wants to feel
"I am here with you",
"I am not going anywhere",
"I will protect you"
"I will provide for you"
"I can stay present with emotion"
"You can rely on me",
"It's me and you in this, babe",
"I've got you."

Deep feminine trust in the masculine that "he has got her" through thick and thin, is a truly sacred quality to embody and be able to offer the feminine. And like most things that are really special and highly valued, it is something that must be earned and demonstrated again and again.

On a scale of 0-10 how much does your partner
feel like you can physically protect her?
On a scale of 0-10 how emotionally
safe and able to stay present with
the full range of her emotions are you?
On the scale of 0-10 how able to
financially provide are you?

FORCED SUBMISSION VS TRUSTING SURRENDER

It may seem easier for you
to try to control her
or force her to submit
and have her regress
by playing a Daddy Doms little girl fetish,
as your way of creating the polarity
of masculine-feminine attraction.

Those games can be fun and sexy
or healing of past unmet needs and traumas,
and are a totally legit form of play.

But it is a very different dynamic
to earn the trust and respect
of an adult feminine woman
who is independent and can take care of herself
but also yearns to be led and directed
with respect, clarity and attunement.

In the potent power of your
embodied masculine presence
she feels so safe and cared for
desirously seduced,
deeper than words
or psychological roles.

There she allows herself
to naturally soften,
relaxing into your strength,
and effortlessly surrenders open,
into her empowered,
receptive
juicy,
feminine,
radiant essence.

Masculine Multi-Orgasmic Mastery

There is a lot more to sex
than releasing tension
or objectifying someone
so you can feel like you are 'winning'
and scoring points for your own ego.

Most guys equate orgasm with ejaculation:
a build to pleasurable climax
before a small release,
an emptying out of the pipes.
For the average lad this is it,
how he thinks about
and does sexual release.

The young buck has a lot more chi energy
and if he is less aware of this vital life force
he may unconsciously squander it
all throughout his life, but especially by
using self-pleasure and sex
as an impulsive stress release.

Many guys don't realize each expulsion
costs him a little of his life force supply.
If only he knew now,
what he'll eventually realize when he's older,
maybe he'd want to learn
to conserve and cultivate his energy
and invest his time and attention
in learning to naturally relax
using healthy lifestyle methods
and elevating sexuality as a portal
to empowerment, mastery and Awakening.

The average man like things to be easy
so when most first hear of
multi-orgasmic, non-ejaculatory sex,
he either quickly dismisses it as too hard,
or shrugs it off as an idealistic impossibility.

For most, while in the heat of the act,
whether with a partner or in solo practice
if he surpasses 90-95% of the way to climax
an expulsion is soon to follow.
As he gets close to that
it starts feeling so good
and the temptation of a quick reward
can be so seductive that
it's easy to give in
and let go in a small release.

With fragile male egos,
few men are humble enough
to be willing to learn something new,
inspired enough to be willing to grow,
and deep enough to pursue greatness.
So, it is a rare and special man,
that is inspired to cultivate
one of the ultimate masculine masteries.

For those who dare try,
first he has to know it's possible
then he has to resolutely decide
and commit to developing it.
Next he needs to practice
strengthening his PC muscle with exercises
or pulling up and stopping the flow when he pees.
He also must open and master his breath
to self regulate and redirect energy
away from overly building up in the pelvis.

In order to fully open these chi channels,
if he has experienced trauma
or has any past sexual shame
still stored in his body,
he may need to release it
to fully activate his multi-o capacity.
So as he opens his energy pathways
he can use his breath and attention
to circulate the energy all throughout
his own body and his partner's.

There are so many practices
he can do by himself, or with another,
and what may initially feel choppy
or like 'doing a technique',
eventually relaxes into mastery
as he learns to retain and circulate without discharge
as he becomes able to go indefinitely
and returns to the connection
with even greater potency and presence.

Now instead of one small release,
if he doesn't 'shoot his shot',
he can now go as long as desired,
have multiple climaxes
up the central channel
with nothing going out,
each bigger and more pleasurable.

His infinite endurance,
pervasive presence and powerful energy
also enables his partner to have numerous
and progressively deeper orgasms
as both of them build and build
more and more energy.

At this point their intention for sex
starts to have a big impact.
Instead of both aiming for a small, quick release
feeling relaxed but drained afterwards,
sex becomes an arena for
deep connection, spiritual practice
and is a great enhancement for both beings

As they allow the energy and love
that flows through all things
to open and circulate
through their hearts and bodies,
as sexing becomes a portal,
the depths of pleasure and presence combine
in circulating, conserving and cultivating energy.
a greater range of states,
openness and deeper connection
"making love" and opening as Awake Love Itself.

Unwavering In Her Many Faces

The dynamic range of your states,
from the closure of a mood,
or the intensity of conflict,
to showering me with adoration,
or at the height of pleasure inside you,
all of your flavors and flow,
whether wife or Life,
allow me to practice,
maintaining presence,
staying open and free,
steady, but not stoic,
composed but feeling deeply,
into myself, you and You,
amidst your many faces,
arising and falling away,
in this one timeless Moment.

In which of her myriad of beautiful
faces do you lose presence?

SHE WANTS TO FEEL YOU, MAN

She wants to feel physically safe with us
in the way we inhabit our bodies, physicality and protection.

She wants to feel emotionally safe with us
in the way we can stay as a grounded spacious presence,
with whatever she is feeling—like a rooted loving oak tree.

She wants to feel the depth of our presence in the
way we listen,
breathing as we look deeply into her without
trying to fix or talk too much.

She wants to feel the integrity and alignment of our
values, words and actions, so she can soften open and trust us.

She wants to feel our commitment to development,
willingness to honestly look inside and do our
inner healing, embodiment, learning, maturation
and eventually for some, Awakening.

She wants to feel our courage to live on purpose and that
process of discovery, development and delivery
of our unique contribution to the world.

She wants to feel the power of our commitment that we are
unafraid to claim and commit fully to our work, to Life
and her in loving relationship.

She wants to feel the solidity of our responsibility and
simultaneously the lightness and playfulness amidst the
engagement of our duties.

She wants to feel the humility of a relaxed, open heart on
top of our grounded, empowered confidence, more than
posturing, stoicism, withholding or pretending to have
it all together.

She wants to feel that our own embodied instinct and heart
is so attuned to ourselves, her and Life, that she can relax
open into her flowing essence and trust our masculine clarity
of direction to lead and guide the both of us together.
She wants to feel through our heart openness how deeply
we uniquely cherish, desire, appreciate and love her—
returning to loving connection, again and again.

She wants to feel that we don't just want to have sex with her
to use her as an object, for a few seconds of releasing tension,
or because it is the only intimate closeness we are capable of.

She wants to feel the full penetration of our presence through
a dynamic range of states from slow and connected to
primal ravishment; that making passionate love is for
ourselves, each other and opening beyond.

And then one day, we may realize that all along, throughout
our entire lives, during all the play and growing up, all the
achievements and accolades, all the tests and challenges,
even all the ways she has been asking us to grow,
were actually the Great She, the Muse Herself, whom she
has been acting as a representative for. She, like all our other
mentors, parents, teachers, coaches have been calling forth our
greatness, inspiring us beyond comfort and convention, to living
our own hero's quest, awakening our greater potential, offering
our lives in service and living the fuller range of our humanity
through our empowered bodies, our loving hearts and the
potency of our presence in the world on behalf of all of us.

The very she we have been dancing with all this time
is actually an emissary of the Big She
seductively beckoning us to open, rise up and enter
in the giving of our greatness to Life Itself.

May we remember that we are all in this together
healing, developing and Awakening
as Life Itself beckons us to evolve.

THE
LOVERS

Remember That Night

Remember that night,
on that magical secluded beach,
illuminated by the full moonlight,
talking for hours under the stars.

We snuggled in the sand
hands sensuously exploring
in the intimate spaces with no words,
lips and tongues find each other kissing–
almost instinctively, in sync.

I carried your beautiful sandy body
down towards the open ocean–
beckoning us to dive in.
Your legs wrapped round my waist,
you held me and my gaze,
wading deeper into the warm waters;
swimming naked with you.

Our primal bodies entangled,
immersed in the magic
of the salty, turquoise sea,
pressing into each other
in blissful embrace,
tides of pleasure,
pulsing in and out.

Lovers loving,
In the flow
of Love Itself.

THE APPROACH

He slowly,
confidently approached
strong and powerful
yet sexy and smooth.
She sensed him, sensing her.
Her body softly shuddered
in anticipatory delight.

Deliberate, he continued toward her,
planting firmly in front.
He paused, bodies inches apart;
she felt him taking all of her in
his potent presence pervading her.

His energy felt good to her
powerful, potent, open.
His body was relaxed
not still carrying
the tension of his day,
his mind was clear,
not distracted in thought.

She craved him to come closer–
her desire drawing him in,
her body overflowing with aliveness,
she opened more to receive him
longing for his touch.
His large hand smoothly slid
beneath her yielding arm,
grabbing her naked back,
as he pulled her in close,
chest against chest
heart open to heart.

He slowly leaned in even closer,
meeting her beautiful face.
Her lips caressing his,
body melting with pleasure
sensuous bliss of immediacy,
so vivid, as if again
for the very first time.

*What would need to happen for you to be
more potent in your presence as you approach
your partner or for her to be more juicy and
responsive as she receives your approach?*

LIFE IS BETTER WITH YOU

I respect our freedom and independence.
It is inspiring how self-reliant you are.
And I appreciate how self aware you are.
But I also like that we get to continue
to know and be known more deeply together.

We can see
parts of each other,
we were previously unaware of.
We have learned how to self-regulate,
we are both good on our own,
but sometimes, we co-regulate
even better, together.
And there is something
many times more potent
that emerges
as we do Life in collaboration.

We both source our own energy from Life
and it's amazing
how we amplify each other
even more.

We both feel love at the core,
even in solitude,
and
we get to practice loving each other,
feeling love for Life
all throughout the day,
and together,
Awakening as Loving Awareness.

It's Okay, Ready When You Are

For me,
loving you,
doesn't start
at some point in the future.

Some of us are wise
beyond our years–
with a brightness cultivated
long before this life.
Each Soul has its own evolution
its pace, path and process,
and it's okay.

And while from one view
it may seem like we,
as companions on the road,
are at different places on the journey,
maybe there's a destiny
that has been drawing us together
for a very, very long time.
And it's okay.

Maybe one of us
is older or younger,
got started later,
came in earlier,
or has done more growth
this time around,
and it's okay.

We're not conventional folks,
with fixed notions of age,
aware only of the physical,
unwilling to grow,
so we're not worried about
"dating someone's potential".
And it's okay.

The bright souls,
the emissaries of possibility,
the ones here to evolve our world
will heal and grow and expand
so much in one lifetime
that conventional limitations
don't necessarily apply.
And it's okay.

So when we do meet,
and I trust Life to orchestrate that,
expect to feel no pressure from me.
Let's remember our agreement,
let's not let 'differences' dissuade us
and let's know we can continue to grow
over the course of our lives together.
Who knows, maybe the roles
were reversed last time?
And it's okay.

Does some part of your being
remember I told you:
no matter how far I had to travel,
no matter how long I had to wait,
I would find you again?
What if loving you
continues from now
and just keeps deepening?
Is that okay with you?

I knew I was destined
for someone incredibly special,
and I am so glad I trusted Life
and waited patiently for you,
Because I kept reminding myself
that it's okay,
I know someday
I'm gonna be with you.

DESIROUS UNFURLING

I want to feel your desire,
your heart's open invitation,
softening,
as it relaxes its guard,
with each deepening breath,
responsive to every touch,
your body's way of revealing
its deepening trust in me
as your beautiful petals unfurl,
and I sense
your yearning readiness
to slowly enter you,
permeating you with love.

Reassurances of a Cunning Linguist

If you ever feel uncomfortable
in the pleasurable ways
I use my tongue,
I'd like to reassure you that
I enjoy it as much as you do.

And reassure you
that I am in no rush.

We can do this
as long as you desire,

And
please know
that it
really
truly
turns me on.

I share this with you,
because I would not want
any of these concerns
to trap you in your mind,
keeping you from
deeply relaxing
and fully enjoying
the juiciness and excitation
of this cunning linguist's
worship and adoration
of every
single
part
of you.

*Are you as generous with your
tongue as your partner would like?*

** for more in-depth insights on this subject
see She Comes First by Ian Kerner*

HOW DID IT GET TO THIS?

It was so good in the beginning,
we were both so open and loving.

We had so much fun,
that rush of excitement
when your messages popped up,
the late night phone calls,
and long seconds in between.

Every kiss felt like a promise.
Lusting to feel your closeness.
We couldn't keep our hands off each other.
Your sweet open heart drawing me in.
I thought it would be like that forever.

How did that,
get to be like this?

We're more like awkward roommates now.
Communication has gotten so bad,
at times a strangely silent struggle,
other times arguing about such stupid stuff.
I hate it that we are so critical of each other,
so impatient and emotionally reactive.
I shut down around you.
You feel distant and closed off.

I don't like what we've become
We hardly connect anymore;
the brief moments
of love we share
aren't nearly enough.

I find myself questioning:
from beautiful beginnings,
and dreams of forever
to closed hearts
in this loveless relating,
how did it get to this?

*Could you and your partner use some professional
support to help you heal repair grow and reopen to love?*

Unrequited Love

I love you so much.
And I have so much love to give,
but I'm aching to know
why you don't love me back
as I love you?

Of course,
I'd much rather feel loving
than closed,
numb,
or indifferent.
But, it is beyond frustrating
and so dissatisfying,
to not have my love reciprocated.

Are you just not that into me?

So Love says:
"Why are you not with someone
who mutually gives and receives love?"
"Is it easier for you to give, than receive?"
"Or do you over-give, so you don't have to receive?"

And then I realize:
it feels so familiar.
Is that how my mom or dad was with me,
not returning my love in-kind?
Oh, unrequited love,
what are you teaching me?

JADED

How did your heart get so jaded?

Who hurt you,
betrayed you,
neglected you,
damaged your trust,
made you think love had to be earned?

How did your heart get so jaded?

And whether the foundational
pains and jades
started with your parents
or happened as an adult
the impact they have had on your heart
and your openness to love,
can be felt.

For what it's worth,
I hope you are able
to polish the jades
and redirect the refractions,
by healing the wounds,
releasing the pain,
reopening your heart,
restoring the radiance of your Soul
and ability to once again
feel the love, joy and
beauties of life.

*Has your heart been jaded and if so, would you like
to heal those traumas and reopen to love?*

Love Making as a Spiritual Practice

> I approach you slowly
> so my system can read you,
> sense you and connect with you.

Sometimes it's hot
to get primal and go faster,
but we're so multi-layered,
that if you really want
the deepest pleasure,
the deepest connection,
and the deepest presence,
you have to go slower
to open and turn me on,
on all levels.

> Our minds think,
> but it's in our bodies
> where we actually register feeling
> pleasure and connection.
> So as we expand beyond
> being only in our minds,
> by relaxing and opening our bodies,
> the more we can enjoy and
> the more of our potential we activate.

Sadly, for some of us
our health has gotten out of balance,
his testosterone low
her hormones imbalanced.
Pain, hurt or trauma,
can also have us closed off
or emotionally numb
to protect ourselves.
And as a result
of being disconnected
from feeling and our bodies,
many of us can't get wet,
can't get there
or can't stay up.

But as we heal past trauma,
feel safe, get healthier,
and learn to be in our bodies,
love-making can become
a source of vital connection and
a portal into infinite depths.

I love the way you approach me,
such a powerful presence,
so grounded and strong,
yet I sense your open heart feeling mine.
And your gaze penetrates
to the center of my being,
like you're looking directly into my Soul.

And I love how embodied you are,
the way you shudder as I come closer,
how you soften and open
as you feel safe and connected,
and how responsive you are
as I slowly kiss and caress
up and down your whole body.

Mmmm, you play me like an instrument,
but it doesn't feel like a performance
or some technique you've memorized,
it's like you are reading me and
guiding me more and more open,
moment to moment.
You are sooo sexy,
and I am so attracted to you right now.

Some stick to the purely physical
or psychological aspects,
which can be amazing
but that's just the tip.
It's easy to get stuck there,
but know that there is so much more.

Our bodies are full of subtle channels
and as they open, our forms fill

with energy and aliveness,
becoming highly attuned instruments
of attraction, pleasure and connection.
Once we begin to connect
and make love in this way,
it becomes more than just a quick release,
a way to work out power dynamics
or our only way of feeling close to someone.

> It's a way
> for the masculine to practice
> being unwavering presence,
> even when things get intense,
> whether in a stressful moment,
> at the height of sexiness
> or in the tension of conflict,
> can we still stay strong,
> hard and integrous,
> yet loving with an open heart.

And it's a way
for the feminine to play
with surrendering and trusting,
in being guided and led,
by you and by Life,
allowing ourselves to feel all the things,
letting them move through us.
The more we soften,
the more we open,
the more juicy we get
and the more the juices get flowing.

> And you are so sexy and beautiful,
> and I am so aroused that
> it would be really easy to lose it here.
> But I've been cultivating these capacities,
> opening my channels and learning to retain.
> So instead of having all the intensity build up
> all in one region and then explode,
> I can use my breath to circulate the energy

up the central channel all throughout my system
and yours, filling us with more and more energy.
without releasing anything.
When mastered we can go as long as we want,
both have multiple climactic crescendos
that build upon each other
getting better and better.

And, I love how you went so slow at first.
You really took the time to connect with me
mentally, emotionally, and spiritually.
And you got all parts of my body activated:
the way your breath moved through your lips
to caress my neck as you kissed me
and how you gently touched my nipples
bringing them to full attention,
artfully making your way to
my belly and inner thighs,
before you even touched me there.
You were looking up at me
as you moved and opening me
with such confidence.
You had me wanting you so bad,
that by the time you finally entered me,
it wasn't long before I was gushing with pleasure.

And as amazing as all that pleasure is,
I love how open I am to you and
how open you are to me and how close we feel.
Cause we know this world is not just
about getting as much pleasure as we can.
It's also about healing and growing,
contributing our purpose and
deepening our capacity to love,
so Love Itself can fill and live through us.

And then in the stillness
at the apex of our loving,
our bodies pause,
our hearts circulating the love
between us as it begins to overflow,

and in that powerful moment
a connection to something greater envelops us.
The edge of our skins blur
into the entirety of the moment
as the aperture of Loving Awareness opens.

    As the love making
    and Love Being continues,
    the sense of selves relax
    until only a Witness remains,
    timeless and ever-present.
    And then in a flash of insight
    even that dissolves,
    as lovers, love making and Love Itself
    become the same unified field,
    not two, Non-Dual.

And this is all part of
love-making as a spiritual practice.
The Love that is the very essence of Life
challenges you and me to grow,
invites us to open,
seduces me together with you
into the sacred portal of sexuality.
And should you desire,
It beckons you to allow pleasure and connection
to activate your greater potential
and open you
as
Love
Itself.

REMIND ME, LOVER

We remind each other
all throughout the day
to stay open
and keep feeling the love
as we dance together
through this Great Mystery
lover, loved & loving as Love.

The Feeling of Being Closer

She feels his presence before his touch.
Her body softening as she feels his breath,
rhythmically caressing her neck.
His face moves alongside hers—
mouth gently grazing her ear.

Whispering softly and deeply,
into the center of her being,
how much he cherishes her,
how he loves feeling so close,
how grateful he is to have found her,
and what an honor it is,
to be loving her, as partners.

Our Embrace

I love the way
you sense me:
deeply, subtly
with such nuance,
yet without touch.

And as you move closer
wrapping your arms
around me when we embrace,
my body melts into
the strength of your frame.

Your open heart sensing mine
as we warmly exchange love,
chest pressing against chest,
our bellies breathing together
as I soften into the safety,
of your potent presence.

Even though my nature
can be so flowy at times,
hugging you centers me
as though I am by a solid oak tree
with roots deep in the Earth.

Yet, what I love most
when we embrace
with such depth,
is the way the sense
of "you" and "me" fades
as we melt into Loving Awareness.

Epic Lovers

I have waited so long for you.
My Soul promised yours,
I would find you,
no matter how long,
nor how far.
I have slayed dragons to get to you*,
in timelines past
and in the in between.**

Life beckoning us in becoming,
activating our greater potentials,
preparing us to meet our match.
Magnetic forces drawing us near;
until we were ready to be reunited
The moment our eyes met, we knew.

And now I get to do Life with you
your Soul and my Soul
playing in these amazing bodies,
learning, and expanding,
healing and Awakening
ourselves and the world,
co-creating life together.
as we are mastering loving
and making love
through infinity—
my epic lover.

** Ken Wilber whispered this to his wife Treya on the way to their wedding
| Grace and Grit by Ken Wilber |*

*** Bardos is a Tibetan term for the realms in between death and life
| Tibetan Book of the Dead |*

EMISSARIES OF EVOLUTIONARY LOVERSHIP

We are here to be ambassadors of love
exemplars of greater human potential
and emissaries of evolutionary partnership.
So we heal, we learn and we grow–
regulating our nervous systems
and activating our energetic systems
as we deepen, expand and Awaken,
so that Life can live and love through us.

May our lives and relationship
be a devotional offering to
evolving what is possible
for the future of humanity
wearing grooves of new possibilities
into the morphic field
of love partnership
here on Earth.

PART 4

THE RELATING

The Bloom of Appreciation

Spontaneous appreciations
for how I see and feel you,
open and amplify
your exquisite radiance,
even more.

I Want To Know You

I really want to know you.
The full range and depth of you,
where you have come from,
where you have been.
How the stream of life
has etched its character into you.
I want to know your challenges and struggles,
I want to know about your triumphs and successes.
Please, tell me what you long for,
what you dream of and
where the whispers from the future
are calling you forward.
I want to know you.

I want to see you as you are;
not as an object, statue, not as a static identity,
but as a living, breathing, dynamic human being.
I want to see even deeper, into the essence of your Soul.
I want to appreciate your beauty
through the whole range of states:
when you are writhing in agony
or in ecstatic pleasure,
when you are beaming joy,
giddy with laughter,
or crying in despair.
I want to see you, naturally,
without make-up
and with the sleep still in your eyes
or all dressed up in a stunning gown.
I want to see you.

I want to listen to you,
to really hear you when you speak.
hear you and understand your world
I want to reflect back what I think you say,
so we never fight over not feeling heard.
I'll show you that that I value your opinion,
I will embrace your perspective
even when it differs from mine.

And may the presence I listen from,
in its openness, safety and curiosity,
allow you to discover even more about yourself.
I want to hear you.

I want to feel you deeply.
I want to know how you feel
the things you really care about
what scares and worries you
and what makes you feel alive.
I want to sense your dynamic expression in its entirety.
way your body moves through the world
the way Life breathes in you.
and when you speak, I want to sense
the feelings beneath your words
I want to feel your heart when you are passionate,
the warmth of your loving, the fire of your rage.
To feel how your care and compassion
radiates toward suffering in the world.
I want to feel you.

I want to penetrate into the depths of your being
sensing how each movement tenses or opens you deeper
at times slow and connected, then wild and free
exploring every, measured inch of your body and beyond.
I want presence to permeate and open us so deeply,
until our minds relax and the edges of our bodies blur,
piercing so profoundly, until
unified Openness remains,
not just in the hazy light of the bedroom,
but radiates throughout our lives.
I want deep presence within you.

Yes, I want to know, hear, see, feel and pervade you.
relating from the freshness of each moment
on an endless discovery into how aliveness
animates you, me, us and the Totality of Now.
I am here to live my purpose and deepen my capacity to love,
to be fully human while wide Awake as Awareness Itself;
and that, I want to do with you, beautiful epic lover.
I want to know you and You, through and through, as we do.

Knowing and Being Known

It is truly amazing
that our Souls
get to inhabit
these incredible bodies.

I cherish the part of us
that yearns to be
deeply seen, felt and heard.

What a gift to know
and to be known
as humans
having a spiritual experience
and I love
that we get to do that
so intimately together.

Aligning As We Go

Did we start off too fast
in this passionate romance
with all its new relationship emotions?

Are we getting lost
in the intoxicating lust,
rapid fire text exchanges
and love bomb barrages?

This feels so good,
and I feel so open with you.
It's easy to say things
in the oxytocin highs,
that we can't follow through on
or that aren't true on all levels.

If we backpedal,
it can create mistrust and heartache.
Our once open hearts recoiling
in confusion and incongruence
when the other suddenly pulls back.
I don't want to hurt you
or get hurt myself..

Primal animals can mate quickly,
as can clever words can easily seduce.
But it takes time to create the safety and trust
and ensuring the mutual alignment
that allows us both to open our
bodies, hearts and Souls
physically, emotionally and energetically
To be able to connect in the depths,
is a sacred process, not to be rushed.

There isn't a set time per se
and some come to clarity
more quickly than others.

But we each have
our own pace and process
of trusting, aligning and opening.
So it's important to me that
we're both on the same page
each major step of the way.
This exploration
is something to be
respected and cherished,
both in the beginning
and throughout the entirety
of this dance we're in.

Whether we go fast or slow
let's check-in and communicate
make sure we are both enjoying
and fully aligned in
this beautiful process
of unfurling,
each layer of our hearts.

Don't Use It Against Me Later

If I openly reveal
my inner world to you,
my thoughts and feelings,
especially my fears and insecurities,
please do not bring it up later
and use it as ammunition against me.

If you take advantage of my vulnerability
it makes me not want to share with you,
which erodes the safety of our bond
and creates distance between us.

When you do honor what I reveal
it's like you're protecting
and caring for my heart.
When you show me that respect,
it helps me trust you
and feel safe to continue
to share my inner world
and deepen in connection with you.
So if you want those things,
don't use it against me later.

Reading Your Reaches

I realized that the ways I reach for connection,
may not be the same way you do.
So, I started to pay more attention
to the subtle nuances of our relating.
And because I cared, I really wanted to know
how you feel loved and connected.

When you approached me
with open arms, asking for a hug
or seductively reached under the covers,
it was obvious that you wanted to directly connect.

But when you asked me "How are you?"
I had to discover that was also your way of
wanting to feel closer and more connected–
by knowing my inner experience
and also revealing yours to me.

And the same was true
for asking about my day:
of course you cared to know
but the details were so important
because it was really about
feeling more connected
by knowing each other
and the things that matter to us.

When you wanted to sit on the couch
at night to talk and cuddle
I'd just want to zone out to some show
or scroll away my feelings.
But now I see through those distractions
and we prioritize our evening connection.

I started to get those things down but,
It took me longer to realize
when you were stressed

you needed a little co-regulating connection,
a hug, a hand hold, a little something just so
you could feel I was there with you.
Or that your emotional reactivity
may have sometimes been frustration
about deeper longings
for more quality time with just us.

When you looked deeply into my eyes
I used to look away in avoidance.
But, I have learned to meet your gaze
as a way of seeing into our depths
and the many levels and layers
of Soul meeting Soul.

We meet in connection in so many ways
co-regulating or relaxing at night.
Flirtation, seduction, and playful exchanges,
all building more chemistry and polarity
and cultivating our on-going romance.

And I love that I get to be the one
whose hand you reach for.
Thank you for being so open and loving
and in doing so, helping me,
deepen my capacity to love.

*What are the ways in which your partner
reaches for connection? Have you asked your
partner if you positively respond most of the
time they reach for connection?*

Same Pattern

Seems like we keep repeating
this same pattern again and again.
I do the thing and then you react.
We both close and disconnect.
Rinse and repeat,
without even knowing.

It seems like such a waste
of our beautiful relationship energy
and all our romantic potential.
There is too much love between us,
to keep burning it up
with this same pattern.

What would need to happen
for me to do some deeper reflection
and become more aware or
work with a body-based therapist
to heal the root cause of this pattern?

Or what would need to happen
for one of us to stay open
when the other does "it" again
neither collapsing
or attacking back?

Instead, we could ask a question
to illuminate the pattern
then notice and name
the defensive protectors
and invite each other
back into vulnerability
and open-hearted connection.

What would need to happen
for an evolutionary moment
to help us integrate this pattern,
be more skillful and
use the energy between us
in ways that are more
loving, joyful and life enhancing?

Avoiding Conflict

You tell yourself,
you're avoiding conflict
by not saying or doing
anything that would
"upset" someone else.

But what about the tension
you create inside yourself
by not acknowledging
your own feelings and views?

You can tell yourself
it's to keep the peace,
but what about the part
that is afraid to lose connection?

Do you realize
the lack of intimacy
with yourself
from the blankness
of the unacknowledged
is what creates the distance
from authentic intimacy
between you and I?

Ironic,
the very thing
you are wanting to avoid
gets created
by the avoidance.

Being skillful
with conflict resolution
and restoring
authentic connection
involves including
others and yourself.

*In what way could you be more skillful in
addressing and resolving conflict?*

Cleaning Up Criticism

We used to be so critical
and it became so pervasive.
We didn't even realize
how often we were doing it.
But we started to notice
that when one of us
spoke critically to the other
we'd either collapse and shut down,
get defensive,
or be aggressive back.

The worst impact was
that we started guarding
and closing our hearts.
So we had to acknowledge
the damage we were doing to each other
and the negative impact
on the quality of
our connection and happiness,
in order to really prioritize
cleaning up the coercive criticism
and make a commitment to stop.

We needed to understand
the importance living
with an open heart.
It's in our hearts' openness
that we are able to openly
give and receive love,
develop spiritually
and experience
joy, passion. gratitude and beauty.

So, now, every single time,
I mean every time
from that point forward,
when either of us was critical

the other would ask
"Was that critical?"
which acted as a pattern interrupt.
If I was dishonest and defensive,
you'd say:
 "Should we pause and come back
when both of us can be honest?"
But if I was truthful and said "yes"
you'd follow up with asking
 "Can you say that in a different way?"
So we'd pause,
take a breath,
reopen our hearts
and I'd either re-say it
in a more kind way
or realize it was better left unsaid
so I'd just say "I love you"
and we would laugh or hug it out.

And it only took
a few, short weeks
for us to clean up
the habit of criticizing.
Now, without all the
negativity in the air flying around
there is so much more space for
humor and playfulness,
safety and vulnerability,
flirtation and attraction,
appreciation and love.

UNDEFENDED OWNERSHIP

Imagine she feels hurt
by something you did,
with tears streaming down
her face, she shares her feelings.
You remain open hearted and undefended,
sensing the hurt she feels in her heart
as the result of your actions.

You do not say
"I'm sorry you feel that way."
Instead,
you simply, clearly and concisely
acknowledge what you did.
With genuine remorse,
looking her in the eyes,
letting her know you
can feel the impact on her heart.

In presence, without words
she directly feels the hurt
in the center of her chest
and with a final release of tears
clears the last of it
with a softening sigh.
You articulate a solution
so it won't happen again.
She melts in your arms
and instead of an argument
or continued disconnection
her trust and respect
for you has strengthened
because of your
undefended ownership.

THE GREAT EMBRACE

We gift each other acceptance;
when you love the parts of me
I have not yet embraced and
when I do the same for you.
It helps us learn to accept
the full depth and range of
ourselves, each other and Life.

Staying open
when it's all good,
bright and shiny,
is much easier.
But it's actually the moments
when we're in pattern
not getting our needs met,
dysregulated and reactive,
or judging our own shadows–
those are the real opportunities
to practice staying open-hearted.

And it's in those moments
when we open deeper
to be sourced by the
warm acceptance
of the Universe's
great embrace
like a infinite blanket
enveloping me and you
with all our parts and wholes
welcoming us back
home to Love.

OPEN WHEN WE GREET

Some partner's greet each other
upon reuniting at the end of the day
and it seems like an automated task
a quick peck on the lips or a heartless hug.
Quickly saluting some lifeless statue
you've saluteddone a thousand times before.

Maybe you were in your mind all day
so now your body's full of stress and tension
or inflamed from poor low quality, processed food
so you can't actually sense the aliveness
of life circulating through your bodies.
Or maybe after too many missed connections
or so many criticisms like micro-aggression daggers
that scarred your hearts which
you've have now closed to protect
so you can no longer feel the Love,
that flows through all things,
openly between your own hearts.

Whatever the cause may be,
it feels like too many couples relate
more like roommates than lovers.
You might wonder how
you've gotten so far away
from the closeness you once shared;
while its too painful for others to look at
so instead you choose to be numb, distant and distracted..
But when you reunite each evening,
you could make , each time different.

As you approach,
your system senses your partner's
grounded in your feet and legs
inhabiting your physicality
with power and strength
with vital, potent energy circulating,

breath effortlessly uninhibited and deep,
loving heart relaxed, warm and open
so that you can feel your love for each other
alive as Life animates you now
and fresh each time you embrace.

And if you ever arrive home
still carrying stress and tension
from earlier in your day,
you pause to clear your energy
move your body or change clothes,
before you re-enter after work.
having invested in learning how
to master your energy and states.

In that way, you return home each day,
greeting each other from presence
and open-hearted love,
as a living embrace
feeling the hug and each other
in a way that each time is different
from the immediacy of the present moment,
where the aliveness of Love lives.

Feeling the Love Underneath

It is so easy
to feel your heart
and when you are being
loving and caring,
in your sweetness
or vulnerably sharing
what you are feeling inside.

But it seems like you
close your heart
when you are
nagging and criticizing,
angry and attacking
or numbing yourself
to avoid feeling something.

I used to think
I needed your heart
to always be open.
Anxiety would rise up
in my heart and gut
when your heart closed.
Until I realized it was
a familiar dynamic
I felt as a kid,
when my parent
closed their heart.

Then in a therapeutic process
I went into the matrix
to meet that younger part.
I empathized with the sadness,
felt and released the anxiety,
and reimprinted an alternate ending
with my younger self
merging into my adult,
both now able to stay
open, feel safe, be relaxed
and still feel the love inside
even when you close.

Now with that integrated,
my adult self can respond
in a very different way
when your heart closes–
no longer codependently tied
to having your heart
have to always be open
for me to be okay.

Of course I prefer when
we are both open-hearted
and we do strive
to live that way overall,
but now my heart can stay open
amidst your occasional closures–
independent of your state.

Plus, my acceptance
and steady openness,
when you do close
makes it a lot easier for you
to reopen and reconnect.

When you are feeling stressed,
my unwavering presence
allows you to co-regulate,
once again finding your
relaxed, centered, openness..

When you shut down,
I can stay open
and be curious about you,
patiently asking
what it's like inside.

And when you try to criticize
I can stay upright
ask if you are being critical
and invite another way.

Best of all, when you are angry
I no longer collapse or fight back
I can stay open and empowered

letting you know "I get that you
feel anger and that's okay."
then meeting your gaze
and calling your name,
reminding you of our shared humanity
as you release and melt into tears
coming closer, softening in my arms
reconnecting our hearts to love.

A much deeper trust develops,
when you feel that I've really "got you"
and can hold you even in some of
our more challenging moments.

And the paradox is that when you close,
instead of quickly and anxiously
forcing you to reopen your heart again,
my practice is to breathe while
staying grounded and centered in presence,
keeping my own heart open,
accepting you and your closure
without needing to change or fix.
All while relaxing open
as Loving Awareness Itself
the infinite unified Space
in which both bodies arise.

And then, only then
do I remind you,
sometimes curiously or gently,
other times with playfulness or seduction
and maybe even firmness, if needed,
to rejoin me in the open-heartedness.

One of my secrets
during an occasional storm
in the face of closure or reactivity
is staying centered, grounded
and open, while simultaneously
I have been feeling the love
and your heart underneath

I remember the deepest of our vows
we made to Awaken together
and to live as open-hearted Love.
So we agreed to help remind each other
to open and reopen again and again–
lovers loving into Loving Awareness.

WHAT REALLY MATTERS

Loving each other,
is not measured,
by the big moments:
the wedding,
that great vacation,
or that one big gift.

It's the small moments,
the spontaneous compliments,
the way he lovingly looks at you,
how she nuzzles her head in your shoulder,
the touch on the small of her back when opening the door,
the quiet way she draws out his deeper wisdom,
the feeling of reconnecting after a conflict,
how you support each other through life's challenges,
the way she inspires him to grow and be better,
the way you get each other beyond words,
that squeeze of your hand at just the right moment,
a subtle, loving reminder that you are not alone,
and the myriad of ways,
you are here for each other,
through it all.

THE
HEALING

Underneath the Layers

You and I
both know,
deep inside,
regardless
of how long it's been
since you've felt it open.
beyond all those layers,
you are really loving
at your core.

When you are ready
to reopen your heart,
as you start unveiling the layers
of your body stored-past
rediscovering the long forgotten gift
of your precious human heart
you might encounter
things you haven't resolved.

You may discover
the aches of past hurts,
fears of being abandoned,
parts that doubt their worthiness,
worries about having, then losing love,
and a myriad of other protective ways
you stay safe
by staying closed
and withholding love.

For some people
it may seem too intense,
it may seem too much,
So they'd rather stay closed off
up in the safe-harbor of their minds.

But if you have the courage
to feel through those overlays
when your heart is open,
that is where you'll find
the love and joy
you've been looking for
all this time.

The Love at the Center

The daggers of hurts you've buried,
the distracted loneliness that seems unbearable,
and the range of feelings you numbed:
all protective acts to help avoid discomfort.
But in their defensive covering,
they obscure your beautiful loving heart.

Will you have the courage
to do your inner work and
release your body-stored past?
Will you heal and reopen your heart,
clearing, one by one,
each of the layers
clouding your heart.

Like the ever-glowing light of the Sun
at the center of our solar system,
the love at the center of your being
is ever shining underneath those layers.

Even when the sky is clouded,
the Sun still shines
like the warm love
beneath those layers.
So if you release the trauma
and relax your protectors,
the obscurations lift,
as the light breaks through,
revealing the love
at the center of your being.

Trauma Healing As a Doorway to Presence

I used to judge myself
for having a busy mind
struggling to stay present,
being easily getting distracted
and getting so triggered by things.

Some guru suggested
it was just my painbody,
I should witness and ignore.
Another said to just focus
on manifesting my future.

Until I realized
if I didn't simultaneously
do my inner healing and growth
then I was actually
spiritual bypassing.

I learned The Body Keeps the Score
of my undigested past,
emotions and trauma
I was unable to process
and release in moment
when they first arose.

So my subconscious mind
hid them in my body
for a time in the future
when I'd be more resourced,
and emotionally intelligent
or finally have a safe connection.

So I started learning
to actually feel my body,
stay present with sensations,
to self-regulate or co-regulate,
to then digest and release
past trauma and emotion.

I still want to manifest the future
and stabilize advanced spiritual states
but now I know,
the deadzones and dissociations
are not obstacles to be avoided–
releasing my body-stored past
is the doorway to greater presence.
My healing and spiritual awakening
are actually both part of the same process
that potentiate and enhance each other.

WHO HURT YOUR HEART?

Because it's been that way for awhile,
it may feel quite "normal" to you:
these layers of protective closure
the scar tissue on top of past wounds
the dampened dispassion,
or the subtle ways you hold back love.

But I am curious to know
who hurt your heart?

And will you allow it
to be felt, healed and released
so you can live once again
with an open heart,
free to feel the love,
the real human connection,
the beauty and the joy,
the passionate aliveness of Life?

EMOTIONAL NEGLECT

On the surface,
I don't know any different.
Using only my mind
to navigate the world.
Didn't even notice
the big blank spot
in the front of my torso.

Buried in my subconscious
the neglect of those first years.
Did they warmly welcome me
when I entered this world at birth?
Could they see my Soul
shining through my infant body?
Could they feel me and connect,
attune to me, sensing my needs,
and did they shine loving care
through their own open hearts?

Still wounded from the neglect
of their own unmet needs,
unknowingly passing on
the same trauma and unlove
they received as kids.

And even if they never heal,
I can release and repair the hurts
soothe the aches of longing,
illuminate and free the patterns
and rewire my missed needs
to finally experience the safety
and secure loving connection
my Soul knows is possible.

DON'T YOU SEE ME?

I was more than
a good little kid,
being loveable
when I was behaving
or doing what you want.

I needed you to receive me;
to love me as I was,
for the essence of my being
in my process of becoming.

As I learned to walk and talk,
express my needs
regulating my emotions
and do all the things.

I wanted you see me
like any kid would,
by mirroring back what you saw,
and helping me know myself.

By reflecting my uniqueness,
illuminating budding strengths
and validating my worthiness,
you would have helped me
me build confidence
and feel loved.

I hoped you'd see me
past my mischief and my moods
even when I was impulsive
or dirty from head to toe.

Beyond the surface layers
I wanted you to see my Soul
and love me through and through.

We, Your Parents, Are Deeply Sorry

Whether we are ever able
to have a real conversation
about the past,
we want you to know,
deep down beyond all of our
pain, patterns and protectors,
that we, your parents,
are deeply sorry.

We acknowledge
the profound impact
we have had on your life,
both positively and negatively.
While we probably provided you
with certain opportunities,
there were also needs we didn't meet.
and other ways we neglected to prepare you.

We are sorry if we did not make you feel safe and protected.
We are sorry if we did not make you feel warmly welcomed
and wanted.
We are sorry if we were not always grounded and centered.
We are sorry if we were not open-hearted and emotionally
available for you.
We are sorry if we did not provide a connection allowing
you to securely bond.
We are sorry if we did not give you enough physical
affection and touch.
We are sorry if we were too smothering or controlling.
We are sorry if we were not always there or abandoned you.
We are sorry for the moments we were not present.
We are sorry if we were not attuned to your state and needs.
We are sorry if we did not listen in ways that made you
feel heard.
We are sorry if we did not see you clearly, deeply and uniquely.
We are sorry if we tried to suppress your voice or autonomy.
We are sorry for times we were inconsistent or unreliable.
We are sorry for all the ways in which we were unskillful as
parents.
We are sorry for all we did or didn't do to stunt your
development.

You might imagine our own parents
gave us what they could,
but they missed some things too.
So while it doesn't excuse our negligence, harm or any ways
we did not support your full and healthy maturation,
we were doing the best we could with what we received
and we are deeply sorry for all the pain, trauma and difficult lessons
that our own missed needs and patterns caused you.

Even if we are not ever able to have this conversation,
because we are no longer physically alive
or not emotionally mature enough to genuinely apologize
to you, we hope the above words can be supportive for your
healing process.

In your own way
and your own timing,
may you heal the wounds,
release the pain and
soften the scars to forgive,
so you can experience
the peace, joy, love and freedom
at the essence of your being.

And though it may be buried deep
under our own wounding and patterns,
on some level we hope
you are able to feel
the love we had for you.

May you heal the wounds,
release the pain and
soften the scars to forgive,
so you can experience
the peace, joy, love and freedom
at the essence of your being.

And though it may be buried deep
under our own wounding and patterns,
on some level we hope
you are able to feel
the love we had for you.

May all beings
be happy, loved and free.

Anxious Attachment Style

Even though I spend a lot of time worrying about my relationships, I deeply accept myself.

Even though part of me feels anxious when you, my partner, are away, I deeply accept myself.

Even though I often check to make sure you really love me, I deeply accept myself.

Even though part of me worries whether you care about me as much as I care about you, I deeply accept myself.

Even though part of me feels anxious that you want to get as close as I do, I deeply accept myself.

Even though part of me feels anxious when your heart is closed I deeply accept myself.

Even though part of me feels anxious when you are unavailable to connect, I deeply accept myself.

Even though part of me has difficulty letting go or ending a relationship, I deeply accept myself.

Even though I sometimes doubt myself or struggle with confidence, I deeply accept myself.

Even though part of me has difficulty being alone, I deeply accept myself.

Even though I worry that you might leave or abandon me, I deeply accept myself.

What would I need to embody to feel securely bonded in my romantic relationship with you?

What would I need to embody to feel relaxed, connected and stable with you, so that I can focus on other important aspects of my life?
What would I need to embody to experience you as emotionally available when I reach for connection and reassurance?

What would I need to embody to feel emotionally close, loved, safe, satisfied and deeply connected to you?

What would I need to embody to feel secure within myself, while also feeling connected to you, when you are away?

What would I need to embody to love myself enough to trust that you do love me or let you go and choose someone else who does?
And anything else that would have me feel more securely attached within myself, to you and to Life Divine, am I unwilling to become aware of and embody?

*This piece was about relationship attachment
style awareness, healing and more secure bonding.
If you would like to learn more about how we bond with
loved ones (Attachment Theory) and takea free assessment,
please visit www.johnnyblackburn.net/attachment-assessment.*

Avoidant Attachment Style

Even though part of me has difficulty trusting and depending on others, I deeply accept myself.

Even though part of me prefers to be independent, self-reliant and tries to not need others, I deeply accept myself.

Even though part of me feels really uncomfortable with neediness or clinginess, I deeply accept myself.

Even though part of me tends to avoid deeper connection, too much eye contact or too much affection, I deeply accept myself.

Even though part of me doesn't feel comfortable being emotionally open or sharing my deeper thoughts and feelings, I deeply accept myself.

Even though when my partner tries to get too close, part of me feels hesitant, nervous or pulls away to maintain a little distance,
I deeply accept myself.

Even though I sometimes limit or avoid sustained closeness and connection, I deeply accept myself.

What would need to happen to release all of the past experiences of pain from my body, when I felt like I could not rely or depend on those who were closest to or caring for me?

What would need to happen to release all of the past experiences of disappointment from my body, when others were not competent and trustable?

What would need to happen to release all of the past experiences of sadness of someone not being available for me in times of need?

What would I need to embody to feel safe to allow myself to depend and rely on you, my romantic partner?

What would I need to embody to feel more trust towards and be able to ask for support from you and the trustworthy people closest to me?

What would I need to embody to accept you as one of my closest confidants and to talk most things over with?

What would I need to embody to be more emotionally available to connect with you and positively respond when you reach for connection?

What would I need to embody to be more emotionally open and sharing my deepest personal thoughts and feelings?

What would I need to embody to be more aware of what I want and need in our connection?

What would I need to embody to feel safe to reach to you for connection in good times or distress?

What would I need to embody to feel free in my life and in our connection?

What would I need to embody to like and want to be committed to you?

What would I need to embody to embrace sustained emotional closeness and connection?

An Apology From Your Masculine Partner

Please allow me
to apologize
for all the moments in the past
when I was unconscious
and inconsiderate of you
in my process of growing up.

I apologize
for being unpresent,
checked out,
distant and withdrawn
distracted on my phone
or not giving you my full attention
so you could feel my loving presence
and how special you are to me.

I apologize
for being closed-hearted
emotionally unavailable,
shielded, numb, guarded,
or all the ways
I avoided connection
and limited our closeness.

I apologize
for poor communication,
all the times I didn't respond,
said I would but didn't call,
or didn't know how
to articulate my feelings.

I apologize
for not learning emotional intelligence,
how to be emotionally vulnerable,
knowing how to name what I was feeling,
self-regulate my own intensity
or stay present with your feelings.

I apologize
for ways I was out of integrity
didn't do what I said I would do
didn't follow through on my commitments
didn't take accountability for my actions
was dishonest or unethical
or was out of alignment with my values.

I apologize
for not accepting you,
making fun of you,
trying to masculinize you,
dismissing your feelings,
trying to fix instead of listen
or ways I didn't let you be you.

I apologize
for not being committed,
being avoidant,
wishy-washy or not fully in,
not being loyal
betraying your trust,
or really being scared of trusting,
opening and letting your love in.

I apologize
for being inconsiderate,
having selfish intentions,
not including your perspective,
not trying to understand you,
or not holding the highest good
for you, me, us and All.

Please forgive me
for anything else
I did or didn't do,
said or didn't say
that in any way
hurt your beautiful, loving heart,
disrespected your humanity
or did anything other than
cherish your Soul.

Please forgive me
for anything else
I did or didn't do,
said or didn't say
that in any way
hurt or disrespected you
or did anything other than
cherish your beautiful loving heart
and sacred Soul.

I am starting to finally realize
that truly apologizing
is not about absolving
my own guilt,
but empathizing,
trying to imagine your world
and the impact I had on you,
so we can begin to repair and renew.

Thank you
for your consummate love,
for believing in us
and for helping me evolve
into a better man.

I am sorry
Please forgive me
Thank you
I love you.

An Apology From Your Feminine Partner

Please allow me
to apologize
for all the moments in the past,
when I was unconscious
with myself, you and us.

I apologize for
nagging, criticizing or complaining
instead of vulnerably acknowledging
the impact, or making a clear request.

I apologize for
being emotionally reactive,
not being more emotionally intelligent,
not taking responsibility for
and feeling my feelings.

I apologize for
being aggressive,
attacking, blaming
or projecting onto you,
instead of vulnerably sharing
what I was feeling as a move to de-escalate
and create connection.

I apologize for
emasculating, shaming
or cutting you down,
instead of knowing when
to be lovingly supportive
versus inspiringly challenging
you to be your best.

I apologize for
withholding love,
withholding affection
or withholding sex,

instead of sharing my feelings
or making a request for what I need.

I apologize for
not supporting you,
your growth
and your mission.

I apologize for
taking you for granted
or not appreciating you
and all that you do.

I apologize for
for overly testing you
and not trusting you
and trusting your direction.

I apologize for
enabling you to be unpresent,
distract yourself, play small
or not approach your greater potential.

Please forgive me
for anything else
I did or didn't do,
said or didn't say
that in any way
hurt or disrespected you
or did anything other than
love, nurture and support
your presence, strength
and full potential of your Soul.

Thank you
for your consummate love,
for believing in us
and for helping me continue
to brighten and deepen
into my radiant loving essence.

I am sorry
Please forgive me.
Thank you.
I love you.

*Is there an opportunity for you to apologize
to your partner for any of these things?*

CAN YOU RECEIVE MY LOVE?

Can you feel
how much I love you;
not just as a concept
in your mind,
but really feel
and receive it
in the center of your chest?

It seems like it's
one of your favorite subjects,
you even have it written
on some of your clothes.
And you have done
all these wellness things
to beautify and adorn your body.
You've worked so hard
almost like you were
trying to earn love
in some future moment.

But here I am,
right in front you,
loyal,
here to stay
and not going away.
So now,
when the love you've said
you've always wanted
is right outside your door,
warmly emanating
out of my open heart;
can you relax open
and let it in?

Reassurance of a Secure Partner

For the part of you,
that sometimes feels anxious
about your relationship connection:

I am here.

You and I are good.

Our bond is secure.

I appreciate you.

I am so attracted to you.

I choose you, and only you.

I like being committed to you.

I want to continue growing and deepening with you.

I am excited to continue building an epic life with you.

And I am not going anywhere.

I love you.

And when this is embodied,
With much more power than words,
the secureness is transmitted in the way
you look at your partner,the relaxation of your
breath,the consistent openness of your heart
and the availability of your presence.

So Safe with You

There are things I share with you,
the best, and worst, aspects of me,
parts unseen, unheard, or unknown
by the likes of almost anyone else.

Your presence,
and the way you,
attentively listen,
not trying to fix,
or problem solve,
nor judging aspects of me,
I am still growing into,
has me feeling so safe,
to reveal myself to you.

Your unwavering centeredness,
relaxed, open and steady
when I am feeling
the full range of emotion,
not uncomfortable
with my distress,
creates safety that allows me
to openly feel with you.

You have accepted parts of me,
that I am still learning to love,
and in that permission to safely unveil,
I am able to discover,
and know even more of "me";
in my radiant brightness,
just as in my moments,
of unconsciousness.

Because I feel so safe with you,
it feels so natural
to want to bare myself to you,
allowing you in even more,

to let you know me,
feel me, and see me,
in the full depth and range:
in my humanness,
my Soul,
and all levels being.

When something positive happens,
you are the first person
I want to celebrate with,
and when
an occasional challenge arises,
it's your hand I want to grab for solace.

When I reach for connection,
I trust you will read it,
respond positively
and meet my desire.
When I need space or solitude,
you understand and are okay.

Neither of us are going anywhere
we can trust and rely on each other,
and I feel you with me,
fully in, ride or die.
As a result of all that goodness,
our bond is a safe haven,
that we return to again and again,
that nourishes, enriches and potentiates us.

From a secure foundation,
we get to enjoy,
all of the sexiness and chemistry
from the polarity of attraction between us
instead of using the anxious-avoidant chase
or trauma bonding
to generate attraction.

And it is from this same secure base,
that we get to play, learn,

heal and grow, and express ,
our unique life purposes,
making passionate love over and over
continuing to relax open our hearts
in mutually reciprocating love
and amplifying it even more
as it emanates
from the essence of our beings,
overflowing and rippling out
to all of Life.
Ever deepening, and savoring it all
as we traverse this miraculous Life
interdependently:
individually, and together.

PART 6

THE
LOVING

THE SCHOOL OF LOVE

Oh Love,
oh how you teach us,
cracking us open
so we can feel.

You invite us on this experiential journey,
embodying the depth and range of loving,
as we give and receive love
encouraging us to be fully in or to let go,
the many ways love lives through us,
You, one of the ultimate teachers.

Traditional education is not for everyone,
but whether we realize it or not,
we are all students
in the Universal School of Love.
Some of us are taking preliminary courses
before getting to experience You and "study" directly.

Some might be working on feeling worthy of opening to love,
others might assume the false belief that they have to earn You
through performance, achievement or being perfect,
before they can open and let You in.
Some stay closed, which inhibits feeling You,
fearing judgment, hurt or rejection.
Others want to let You In,
but still fear you might go away if they do.

Passing through these processes of admittance
once they are accepted to the School of Love,
looking back on what it took to get here
there were times it may have felt difficult,
challenging, or even daunting to be with the fear.
There may have been feelings
of not-enoughness and shame
that held us back from the simple act
of opening the door of the heart to love.

Once we're in the School
or rather, we let You into our hearts,
We can choose our own study path.
One course is about
learning to give love to others,
to friends, loved ones, and eventually
in the advanced levels, all living beings.
Another is receiving love and letting it in
compliments, touch, support and even pleasure.
Naturally, learning self-love is an essential foundation
that every student has opportunities to learn.

Then there is learning to love while being "fully in"
secure, openly available, reliable and committed.
And finally, comes letting go—
allowing the process and fully feeling the grief
of losing a part of you, love, from one of your forms.
Sometimes a special course is needed to help
heal, restore, forgive and reopen the heart after being
hurt, betrayed, abandoned or jaded in love.

And lastly, there is the advanced course,
Awakening as Loving Awareness
For much of the School's history
few students at the Earth campus
have been interested in this One.
But, we are living in exciting times,
more and more are getting sneak peaks
and wanting to deeply dedicate to Its study.

And You, one of our greatest teachers,
in your wisdom, You make the learning so immersive
that most of us don't even know
we are in School, this thing we call Life,
deepening our capacity to love
in all these beautiful forms.

What is one of the aspects of love you are learning about?

Layers of Love

In healing the neglect of my younger years,
I learned to love myself.

In the dance of our romantic lovership,
I've become able to love another.

And in my surrender to Life,
the sense of "I" relaxes to be Awake as Love Itself.

Can I Keep My Heart Open?

Can I keep my heart open and love you?

Can I keep my heart open when you feel sad?

Can I keep my heart open when you feel moody or blah?

Can I keep my heart open when you don't feel pretty?

Can I keep my heart open when you worry you have gained a few pounds or feel bloated?

Can I keep my heart open when you worry you are getting old or losing your beauty?

Can I keep my heart open when you don't forgive yourself?

Can I keep my heart open when you feel ashamed?

Can I keep my heart open when you feel anxious about our connection?

Can I keep my heart open when you close your heart?

Can I keep my heart open when you have difficulty receiving and letting love in?

Can I love and accept the parts of you that you try to hide or don't yet love?

Can I stand in presence, when you feel upset, and feel with you—grounded, relaxed breathing, heart open, not needing to change or fix, accepting you as you are?

Can I keep my heart open and powerfully pervade you with masculine presence as we make passionate love?

Can I still see your beauty, love and adore you, however the
light shines through you?

Can I remember it is not about perfection, but about
practicing opening and reopening our hearts?

Can I keep my heart open and love you over and over
until we love and accept
everything so deeply,
we open as Loving Awareness Itself?

*What is one dynamic with your partner
in which you can practice keeping your heart open??*

SEEN & STILL LOVED

That I even feel safe enough
to reveal myself to you
naked,
so you
can see me
is so special.

But, that you
have seen my flaws,
and still accept me
continue to love me
just the same
is one of the things
that makes you
so extraordinary.

FALLING?

Have you ever wondered why they say "falling in love"?

Maybe it is because the common protectors
that guard our heart and have many people
living with a closed heart most of the time.

But in the initial feelings of excitement
with all the new relationship emotions,
with that new special connection,
the overwhelming flood of chemistry,
knocks down those otherwise strong sentries
who normally protect our vulnerability,
and now allows the experience of being open-hearted
which can feel like "losing control" or "falling".

And so in the beginning of this honeymoon phase
as our hearts are more open
we can experience more of our
open-heartedness potential
which could be our natural state of being
with friends, loved ones and all throughout our lives.

So the more we learn to live with an open heart,
love ourselves and be in love with life,
whether we are in partnership or not,
the more we can feel the various forms of "love"
desire sexual to divine (eros),
playful love (ludus),
obsessive love (mania),
soul connection (philia),
devotional love (storge),
mature love (pragma),
self-love (philautia),
universal love (agape).
and Awake Love (Loving Awareness).
The more the love that animates all things
can openly flow in and out of our hearts.

So then when we do meet an extraordinary person
we no longer fall head over heels,
dropping our protective guards
and losing ourselves in each other.
Instead, we activate each other even more,
amplifying the love at each of our centers,
many times greater than on our own.
We inspire, support and adore each other,
and we have each other's back 100%.
The secureness of our beautiful bond
creates a grounded stability
that makes everything in our lives even better.
And from this safe and solid base
we get to create an on-going romance
and whether making love
or re-opening after a conflict,
we are practicing loving ourselves,
each other and the Life Divine in all its forms.

So what at first felt like falling,
now feels more like expanding.

The Heart Questions

Ask yourself:

"Is my heart open?"

"Am I being Loving?"

"Can 'I' relax Open as
Loving Awareness?"

Our Precious Human Heart

In the tenderness of our heart,
shields defend us from judgment,
protective walls guard us from hurt,
veils hide us from being seen and
hurt pains us when unloved or unimportant.

In the fear and doubt in our heart,
we slink with hesitance and shyness,
checking if it's really safe to open.
Am I safe, special and do you care?
Will you go away or be there when I reach?

In the confusion of our heart,
we can send mixed signals:
when depressed, we might be
numbing to avoid feeling,
when we're loud, we could
want attention and connection,
when aggressive, we may be
protecting fear or shame underneath,
when pretending not to need others,
we might be scared of trusting.

In the beautiful openness of our heart,
I feel connection with others,
I can give and receive love,
I feel gratitude beauty and awe,
I radiate joy and exude passion.

In the genuine curiosity of our heart,
my heart wants to connect with you,
my heart wants to see you,
my heart wants to feel you,
my heart wants to know you.

In the security of our heart,
we trust we can rely and

depend on close connection,
we are here for each other
when we reach out,
we can thrive in our bond
and as sovereign individuals,
we can enjoy and savor life,
making love amidst it All.

In the humility of our heart:
we can apologize when off or out of integrity,
we can allow devotion to pour through,
we can bow down and surrender to the Divine,
we can dedicate our life to being of service.

In the Awakening of Big Heart:
practicing opening and loving,
over and over
compassion and integration
of light and dark,
expanding our span of justice,
care and equality
more love and positive regard
for all of Life.

In the sacred portal of the heart:
doorway to Infinite Unified Seamlessness,
feeling Love as the Fabric of Reality,
the Essence that has been here all along,
we just had to relax open to feel It.

One or Oneness

I thought that in love,
me plus you,
one plus one equaled one.
But I realized that
I was merging with you,
losing myself in relationship,
just like when I was an infant,
fused with mother, without identity.

So, I learned to stay in my center
while connecting even deeper with you.
I discovered taking care of myself
and having healthy boundaries
was being considerate of me and you.
Now you plus me equals we.

Releasing old, body-stored shame,
and developing a better integration of my parts,
builds confidence and freedom.

All this before learning
to relax the identity—
like opening the door
to an authentic uniqueness
simultaneously sourced
from identityless Infinity.

So I guess,
one plus one
does equal One...ness.

A Feeling & Everything

To all the lovers out there,
may we remember that love
is not just a mental concept,
but the direct experience
of feeling a warm emanation
in the center of our chest.
And when our hearts are open,
it can be given and received,
self-sourced from Life
or exchanged with others.

And so,
our romantic partnership
and every moment of our lives,
are opportunities to live
with an open heart
loving ourselves, each other and all of Life.
And may we continue opening
our hearts again and again,
loving as a feeling with a lower- case "l"
until relaxing and expanding open
as the Big Love, with a capital "L",
the very fabric of existence,
forms and formless co-arising
human love and Love.

Ambassadors of Love

When our hearts are closed,
disconnected from feeling
the aliveness and Love
that lives through all things,
it's easy to get lost
in the trivialities of society.

It just so happens,
that there are loving emissaries
alive on this Earth
whose open hearts
allow the Love,
which is the Essence of Life,
to shine and flow through them.

These Ambassadors of Love,
in allowing their lives
to be animated by Love,
naturally inspire, invite and ignite
others to relax open their hearts
so they too can feel and emanate the Love.

In this way, living with an open heart
sends out positive ripples
toward the healing, betterment
and Awakening of our world
one candle lighting another
until the whole Earth is illuminated.

PART 7

AWAKE LOVE

THE WORLDS WITHIN

In your quiet interior,
beneath the skin,
beyond the projections
of how you want to be known
lie inner realms unseen.

Emergent upwellings
on this tapestry of aliveness,
thoughts and sensations,
energy and emotion,
pains of the past,
whispers of the future,
echoes of the Eternal,
worlds within worlds.

Arising and falling away,
each moment anew.
You just gotta be willing
to pause and be still,
surrender to Presence,
feel the Love and
be the Space,
as the Universe unfurls.

Undefended Love

Guarded heart,
closed and bracing,
protecting shields,
numbing from feeling,
scars of hurt and pain,
can't feel anything
and love can't get in.

Undefended heart,
naked and alive,
unobscured feeling,
sensing and breathing life,
giving and receiving love,
opening and reopening,
again and again.

Practicing loving
until Big Heart Opens,
that which feels the
Great Openness of Love,
Awake as All Things.

Loving the Shape of You

I am loving

the shape of you

while relaxing open

as the shapelessness of YOU.

BEAUTY, YOU WITHIN YOU

As I am gazing into your eyes,
beyond the color and shape
the depth of your feeling
reveals itself to me.
And if I allow the looking
to go even deeper,
beyond the patterns and personality,
into the truer depths of your being,
unveiling the essence of your Soul
shining through to me.

The functions of seeing and sensing blur
beyond body and Soul
as the aperture of Awareness opens
and it's from this view,
I experience your deepest beauty
amidst the infinite backdrop
of Radiance Herself
emanating from
the heart of Life,
co-arising as
you within You.

OPEN & OPEN

When my heart is open,
I can feel the joy and beauty of life.

When our hearts are open,
we can feel our love for each other
and the security of our bond.

When the Big Heart is wide open,
the Love that flows through All Things
is felt as the fabric of our Being.

In this way, we remind each other
of the love you and I share,
as well as the Love we All are.

DEPTH OF LOVE

The deepest states of love
are ineffable,
wordless,
just like I Am,
where the sense of me relaxes
and the edges of my skin blur.

It is a Space
without location,
to which concepts can only point,
and where Love is the deepest Reality.
It is the field, my love,
meet me there.

THE MOST REAL

Love can seem so intangible,
but when
it's flowing through
my open heart,
it feels like
the most real,
the most essential,
the substance of Life,
like my body and yours,
like the Earth and the stars,
the very fabric of the Universe
are made of Love.

Turning Towards the Source

In the center of your chest,
beyond the hurts and protectors
all hearts want to open to Life.

Will you allow yours to relax?

Unfurl its guardian petals
like a flower instinctively turning
towards the light of the Sun,
blooming open to reveal the Love.

That which you've been seeking,
has been inside all along.

I Want Both of Us to Feel You

We thought it was just the two of us living together;
cooking, cleaning and doing all the things.
All so mundane, stuck in our minds,
so we couldn't feel anything.

Until the first time we glimpsed You.
Thoughts went quiet, selves relaxed,
Awareness expanded and there You were,
everything, everywhere, all at once.

Your first visit was short, but it left us in awe.
longing to feel Your Presence again,
more beautiful and real than anything else;
that one taste igniting an unquenchable thirst.

So, we stopped mindlessly watching screens
and distracting ourselves on our phones.
Sometimes we sat in silent stillness, inviting You in.
We started naturally keeping our home cleaner,
so it could be a sanctuary worthy of You.

Instead of dreading chores
or being partially engaged in tasks,
we started actually wanting to do
exactly what we were doing,
fully engaged in the activity at hand,
which ushered us into Flow states
and there You were again.

Opening our hearts
we added joy to the cooking
took pride in the cleaning and
spontaneously danced around the house
and when we did things with spirit,
You often came to visit.

Couch conversations became a portal
into deeper intimacy with each other
and You were right there with us.
And when we made love
it became an offering to You,
an invocation that You'd open us,
animate us and love through us.

After that first visit, we felt so sad
when we thought You'd left.
Silly us, we didn't yet realize
You'd had been all around
and with us all along,
but we just weren't
open enough to feel You.

But gradually we got more glimpses,
Your visits became longer and stronger,
until we could feel Your Presence all the time.
Opening and reopening again and again
loving so deeply until we
became You, Love Itself.

** inspired by the Hafiz poem "I Want Both of Us"*

LOOKING THROUGH ALL OUR EYES

She knew, he knew,
that when, trustingly,
she allowed him
to peer inside her,
to be seen, felt and known
through the openness
of her beautiful, loving heart,
that he held these moments
in the intimate richness of immediacy
as precious gifts given freely
amidst the momentariness of Life.

And it was in these moments
she sensed
in the depth of his presence
in an undefinable,
yet oh so palpable way.
like the most real thing in the world,
Loving Awareness Itself,
that which looks through all our eyes,
looking and sensing through him.

Loving Open as Love

Deep down,
your Soul remembers
part of why you are here
is to give and receive love
and in the loving,
to relax Open
as Loving Awareness.

THE NATURE OF YOU

Imagining what it was like
to be in the soul skin of John Muir
his fascination to explore You,
championing your wildness,
his deep respect for You:
appreciating Your beauty
in all Your many forms.

As the running water,
ever ebbing and flowing
multitudes of emotional waves,
etching their character
in the unique topography
of your beautiful face.

But beyond your cycles of seasons
or your flux of ever changing states
there is something unchanging,
some same Essence,
shining through
Your True Nature.

PRESENCE & LOVE IN ALL THE THINGS

May he cultivate his attention
so that he is fully engaged
in whatever is being done.

And may the potency
of his presence
penetrate her
through the depths
of her being
and beyond,
as she overflows
with sensuous desire
and deep devotion
in loving
herself, him
and All Things.

Creatures in the Vastness

Such small creatures
we humans are
in this vast Expanse,
99% empty space.

Does nothing really matter?
Are we just
meaning-making machines
imprisoning ourselves
with our own social constructions?
Or is it all some illusory Samsara?

It's easy to be resigned,
get lost in nihilistic pessimism
or become disheartened.
Until the heart relaxes open
and Awareness expands
to actually feel
the Love that fills
the empty Vastness.

Great unifying force,
intangible fabric of Reality,
seemingly tangible emanations,
the eternal transmigration
of ever-changing matter—
arising and falling away.
Form out of the emptiness,
empty essentially are the forms—
two sides of the same coin.
Yet it is Love that animates
these creatures in the Vastness.

** inspired by Only Through Love*
"for small creatures such as we, the vastness
is bearable only through love"
—— Carl Sagan ——

LONG LOVING LOVERS

Long loving lovers
is not about
two humans
in a love making marathon
for countless hours
or staying alive and married
for thousands of years.

Eventually,
some may realize,
in the many moments
through the many forms,
that You
have been inviting us,
through our hearts and bodies,
in all our relationships
beyond person, place and time
and into the Great Chain
of Being and Becoming:
lovers, loving into Love—
the Eternal Loving.

Gratitude & Acknowledgements

Thank you to all the people and experiences that have helped, empowered and inspired me to embody my greater potential and deepen my capacity to love past, present and future.

Special thanks to Matt Kreinheder, William Potter, Josh Macin, Krista Richards, Alex Regalbuto, Izzy Ivy, Jason Hernstad, Carole Griggs, Allen Bittaker, Laura Styler, Cedric Winterwolf, Michele Rooney, Koichi Naruishi, James Cruzen, Caroline Mayou, Pete Kirshmer, Jess Magic, James Applington, Viraja Prema, Alix Tingle, Josh Trent, Silvia Souders, Fernando Mercado, Willow Brown, Kai Van Bodhi, Apryl Stephenson, Chris Maher, Anna Jackson, Guy White, Lauren Peters, Tobin Wolfe, Teresa Mutch, Eli Call, Katia Diamond, Daniel Bradley, Lindsay McCarthy, David Beaudry, Keri Nola, Brent Kozlowski, Catherine Garceau, Lloyd Laperdon and Jeffrey Platts for your friendship and all the epic conversations about growth, healing, embodiment, masculine and feminine polarity, attachment, authentic relating, sacred sexuality, evolutionary love and Awakening.

Deep gratitude to Raina DeLear, Annalisa Aldeberg, Frank Carucci, Thomas Hubl, Dustin Diperna, James Baye, Laura Divine, Joanne Hunt and Bonnie Grossman for your wisdom, inspiration, healing and guidance.

Thank you Anastasia Smith, Aiganym Tynysbayeva, Drisana Carey, Komala Saunders, Sonia Reece, Sarah Speers, Kat Muller, Niki Van Houten and Katrina Carroll for your heartfelt devotion, help and service.

Lastly, heartfelt gratitude to my family: Shannon, Beckett, Bronson, Vern, Mom, Dad, Valeta, Michael, Aubrey, grandparents, aunts, uncles and cousins for your consummate love, laughter and support.

In loving gratitude,

Johnny

About the Author

Johnny Blackburn is a contemporary mystic and a well-respected authority on human development, embodiment. and the Spiritual Awakening process. He is the founder and director of Mystics, a modern school with an integral approach to embodied healing and full-spectrum development, and whole human Awakening.

With an original background in Management Consulting and an Undergraduate degree in Business from the University of Southern California, a life-changing injury and failed surgery profoundly altered the course of his life. At the worst, confined to the floor for 22 hours a day, Johnny spent 2 years reading, meditating and healing himself from all angles. After a full recovery, a new path revealed itself. Having emerged from the transformative chrysalis, Johnny continued developing through inner cultivation. He earned a Master's Degree in Psychology, in addition to innumerable multi-disciplinary trainings, embracing diverse fields of study to enrich his understanding, broaden his perspective and deepen his skills.

In 2010, Johnny has more than 10,000+ client-coaching hours counseling individuals and couples, facilitated hundreds of hours of groups and led dozens of retreats in Southern California, as well as all over the world. Johnny Blackburn serves as a catalyst for activating leaders, who themselves are healing heal and empower their own clients and communities, creating a ripple effect of positive change. He serves a range of entrepreneurs and change makers, executives and working professionals, and loving couples.

His work serves as a bridge between the perennial spiritual insights of wisdom traditions across time with the leading psychological research on adult human development and the upper reaches of human potential. Standing on the shoulder's of giants, Johnny and other leaders humbly continue to carry this torch, illuminating our way forward as we continue to evolve toward betterment of Life on this wondrous Planet.